CONTEMPORARY PERSPECTIVES *on* LITERACY

Mastering
GLOBAL
LITERACY

Heidi Hayes Jacobs
SERIES EDITOR

Veronica BOIX MANSILLA
Anthony W. JACKSON
Heidi Hayes JACOBS
William KIST
Homa Sabet TAVANGAR
Silvia Rosenthal TOLISANO

Solution Tree | Press

a division of

Solution Tree

555 North Morton Street
Bloomington, IN 47404
800.733.6786 (toll free) / 812.336.7700
FAX: 812.336.7790
email: info@solution-tree.com
solution-tree.com

Visit **go.solution-tree.com/21stcenturyskills** to find direct links to the many tools and resources cited in this book.

Printed in the United States of America

17 16 15 14 13   1 2 3 4 5

Library of Congress Cataloging-in-Publication Data

Mansilla, Veronica Boix.
  Mastering global literacy / Veronica Boix Mansilla [and five others].
    pages cm
  Includes bibliographical references and index.
  ISBN 978-1-936764-58-7 (perfect bound) 1. Literacy programs. I. Title.
  LC149.M267 2014
  302.2'244--dc23
                          2013036098

Solution Tree
Jeffrey C. Jones, CEO
Edmund M. Ackerman, President

Solution Tree Press
President: Douglas M. Rife
Editorial Director: Lesley Bolton
Managing Production Editor: Caroline Weiss
Senior Production Editor: Suzanne Kraszewski
Copy Editor: Sarah Payne-Mills
Proofreader: Elisabeth Abrams
Cover Designer: Jenn Taylor
Text Designer: Laura Kagemann

The *Contemporary Perspectives on Literacy* series is dedicated to Jane Bullowa, former assistant superintendent for instructional services at the Ulster Board of Cooperative Educational Services in upstate New York where she worked for thirty-seven years. It has been my experience that regional service center leaders are among the most talented and forward-thinking educators in the United States. In that tradition, Jane was relentlessly progressive yet had the easiest style. She encouraged innovation and provided educators with opportunities to try out new approaches. In particular, she prompted me to engage in the integration of emerging technologies from the onset of the first CD-ROMs to Netscape Navigator as a browser. I vividly remember the day she introduced me to my first videoconference on a Polycom, and I could see the world expanding in our classrooms. Jane opened learning portals for thousands of students, teachers, and administrators. Thank you, Jane.

—Heidi Hayes Jacobs

Acknowledgments

The process of writing a book is both personal and collaborative. Many individuals contributed to this series, bit by bit, page by page, experience by experience. I want to start with a deeply felt thank you to our chapter authors. Each one of them juggles multiple responsibilities, and I value and appreciate the time and effort each has invested in reflecting on, wrestling with, and defining the new literacies.

In two memorable conversations—one in Melbourne, Australia, and one in San Francisco, California—Douglas Rife, president of Solution Tree Press, prompted me to consider creating the four-book series *Contemporary Perspectives on Literacy*. I am grateful for the personal encouragement and coaching he has provided while concurrently displaying remarkable patience. Outside reviewers, under the direction of Solution Tree Press, gave us solid and incisive feedback on our first drafts that helped our authors rework and craft their text. The editorial staff at Solution Tree Press is of the highest quality, and we continue to appreciate their direction.

Countless numbers of teachers and administrators from around the world work diligently to bring the best to their students every day, and they have provided inspiration for our work at the Curriculum 21 Project. The Curriculum 21 faculty—a group of exceptional professionals—has been supporting educators since the early 2000s. They are an inspiration and a testament to the power of collaboration.

In particular, I want to give a round of applause to Elisa Black and Kathy Scoli for their outstanding and meticulous editorial work preparing chapters for review. Justin Fleisher and Michele Griffin were extremely helpful in assisting me with the research for chapter 4, "Designing a Film Study Curriculum and Canon," in *Mastering Media Literacy*. Earl Nicholas proved to be a constant anchor and creative soundboard in projects related to merging curriculum and technology.

With constant support and humor, my husband, Jeffrey, is always there for me when I take the plunge into a new project. As always, our adult children, Rebecca and Matt, are my ultimate inspiration.

—Heidi Hayes Jacobs, Series Editor

Solution Tree Press would like to thank the following reviewers:

Michele C. Crowley
French Teacher
George H. Moody Middle School
Henrico, Virginia

Kim Hollis
International Baccalaureate Programme Coordinator
Allen D. Nease High School
Ponte Vedra, Florida

Elizabeth Thorne-Wallington
PhD Candidate, Department of Education
Washington University in St. Louis
St. Louis, Missouri

John Wheeler
Principal
Cedar Ridge High School
Hillsborough, North Carolina

Visit **go.solution-tree.com/21stcenturyskills** to find direct links to the many tools and resources cited in this book.

Table of Contents

Chapter 5. Interdisciplinary Global Issues: A Curriculum for the 21st Century Learner

By Heidi Hayes Jacobs

About the Series Editor

Heidi Hayes Jacobs, EdD, is an internationally recognized expert in the fields of curriculum and instruction. She writes and consults on issues and practices pertaining to curriculum mapping, dynamic instruction, and 21st century strategic planning. She is president of Curriculum Designers and director of the Curriculum 21 Project, whose faculty provides professional development services and support to schools and education organizations. Featured prominently as a speaker at conferences, at workshops, and on webinars, Heidi is noted for her engaging, provocative, and forward-thinking presentations. She has published eleven books, as well as journal articles, online media, and software platforms. Above all, Heidi views her profession as grounded in a K–12 perspective thanks to her early years as a high school, middle school, and elementary teacher in Utah, Massachusetts, Connecticut, and New York.

Heidi completed her doctoral work at Columbia University's Teachers College, where she studied under a national Graduate Leadership Fellowship from the U.S. Department of Education. Her master's degree is from the University of Massachusetts Amherst, and she did her undergraduate studies at the University of Utah. She is married, has two adult children, and lives in Rye, New York.

To learn more about Heidi's work, visit www.curriculum21.com and follow her on Twitter @curriculum21 and @heidihayesjacob. To book Heidi Hayes Jacobs for professional development, contact pd@solution-tree.com.

Introduction

By Heidi Hayes Jacobs

To many of us, the label *21st century* conjures up visions of futuristic scenes from Isaac Asimov's writings. Indeed, labeling global, media, and digital literacies as *21st century skills* is a misnomer. In reality, these are *right now* proficiencies—*new literacies*. Even though the future has caught up with us, and the 21st century is right now, we continue to serve students in school systems that operate on a 19th century timetable and deliver a 20th century curriculum. To reference another futuristic author, our education system functions like a Jules Verne time machine, forcing our students to be time travelers between the present and the past.

Nostalgia for the good old days is pervasive in pockets of society, but it is hard to make a convincing case for going backward in the field of education. In my work with U.S. and international schools, I rarely encounter questions about whether or not we should modernize our education system; the pertinent questions are about *how* we should modernize our education system. Grappling with these questions invariably leads to discussion of three new literacies that exponentially empower us to communicate and create with immediacy: global literacy, media literacy, and digital literacy. The *Contemporary Perspectives on Literacy* four-book series is a place to cultivate the discussion of these new literacies.

There are five primary purposes of the series:

1. To clarify each new literacy in order to provide a basis for curriculum and instructional decision making

2. To find the relationship between traditional print and visual literacy and the three new literacies

3. To provide steps and resources to support the cultivation of each literacy in classrooms and virtual learning environments

4. To identify steps and examples of how to lead the transition from older paradigms to the integration of the three literacies in professional development

5. To inform decision makers on the far-reaching effects of policy and organizational structures on the effective modernization of learning environments

A range of perspectives is essential when examining each literacy and how it interacts with others. To that end, the series includes a cohort of writers from a variety of organizations and disciplines—a classroom teacher, a public school district information technology director, a leadership team from an international school, researchers, university professors, the director of a not-for-profit organization devoted to journalism, the founder of an education network, a media critic, a regional service center professional developer, consultants, the leader of a film- and media-making center, and the director of an international society supporting global learning. This team of authors has come together to share views and experiences with the central goal of expanding and contributing to the practice of educators. The commitment of each author to this work is commendable, and I am grateful for their patience and productivity. Working with them has been a remarkable journey.

In this book series, we consider the distinctive characteristics of each new literacy and how schools can integrate them. The new literacies provide exciting possibilities for classrooms, schools, organizations, and social networks. In this book, *Mastering Global Literacy*, we explore how educators seek to cultivate globally literate learners. In the 21st century, the portals of the classroom are wide open as educators both let the world in and seek out new experiences with their learners. However, what does global competency look like? How do we employ new digital tools to connect effectively with other classrooms? How can we localize and personalize the global? What is it like to grow up in a global classroom? What global issues are learners grappling with?

In this book, we begin with the thoughtful and inspired work of Veronica Boix Mansilla from Harvard University and Anthony W. Jackson from the Asia Society. In chapter 1, "Educating for Global Competence: Redefining Learning for an Interconnected World," you will learn about the work of the Council of Chief State School Officers (CCSSO) that produced four teachable and accessible global competencies and how you can integrate these competencies in classrooms.

Chapter 2, "The Globally Connected Educator: Talking to the World—Not Just About the World," is packed with specific programs, methods, and ideas to help any teacher at any level build a bridge between his or her classroom and the world. Born in Germany, raised in Argentina, a teacher in Florida, and en route to a new position in Brazil, Silvia Rosenthal Tolisano is the epitome of the global teacher, but it is not only her personal bio that makes her so. She knows how to connect her learners.

William Kist from Kent State University brings his fascinating work with teachers and how they globalize their classrooms to the foreground in chapter 3, "Taking the Global and Making It Local: A Qualitative Study."

Born in Iran, Homa Sabet Tavangar has a strong commitment to helping teachers make the adjustment from a closed to a global learning environment. She lays out the elements for creating a global classroom and inspires our children to make friends with others in the world in chapter 4, "Growing Up in a Global Classroom."

Curriculum writers are concerned with basic questions about what content, topics, and materials are pertinent to support globally literate learners. The book closes with my chapter, "Interdisciplinary Global Issues: A Curriculum for the 21st Century Learner." I make the case that all problems and issues facing our contemporary learners are inherently interdisciplinary and that we need to make adjustments in our school curriculum to identify and address these issues. This chapter includes criteria for making these choices and a sample set of possible units.

We hope that these five chapters will bring different perspectives to the dialogue regarding how to support the shift to new types of learning environments that can integrate digital, media, and global literacy into organizations, teaching practice, administrative styles, and ultimately, into the lives of learners.

We encourage you to connect *Mastering Global Literacy* with the other three companion books in the series for a more complete and detailed examination of the new literacies.

Visit **go.solution-tree.com/21stcenturyskills** to find direct links to the many tools and resources cited in this book.

Veronica Boix Mansilla is principal investigator for Project Zero's Interdisciplinary and Global Studies Project at Harvard Graduate School of Education and a Bernard Schwartz Fellow at the Asia Society. Her research examines the conditions that enable experts and young learners to produce quality interdisciplinary work addressing problems of contemporary significance. Veronica's research focuses on developing and nurturing an informed global consciousness among youth in North America, Wales, and India. With her team, she brings together theories and methods in cognitive psychology, epistemology, pedagogy, and sociology to explore how experts, teachers, and K–16 students advance interdisciplinary understanding of topics of global significance, from globalization to climate change and bioethics.

Veronica chairs the Future of Learning Institute at Harvard and is the founder of L@titud. She has taught at the University of Buenos Aires and the Harvard Graduate School of Education. Veronica is the coauthor of *Teaching for Interdisciplinary Understanding in the International Baccalaureate Middle Years Programme* (2010); *Educating for Global Competence: Preparing Our Youth to Engage the World* (2011); and *The Point of Integration: Pivotal Reflections on Quality Contemporary Interdisciplinarity* (manuscript in preparation).

Anthony W. Jackson is vice president for education at the Asia Society, which works to integrate knowledge about Asia and the world as a mainstay of U.S. education. Since 2005, he has led the development of the Asia Society's International Studies Schools Network, an effort to create a network of small, effective, internationally themed secondary schools across the United States. Before joining the Asia Society, he was a director of the Walt Disney Company's Disney Learning Partnership. Trained in both developmental psychology and education, Anthony is one of the leading U.S. experts on secondary school reform and adolescent development. He worked on Capitol Hill as a senior staff member on the Select Committee on Children, Youth, and Families and later directed the Carnegie Corporation Task Force on the Education of Young Adolescents, which produced the ground-breaking report *Turning Points*. He also coauthored the follow-up blueprint *Turning Points 2000*, which transformed many of the design principles in the original report into concrete action steps for new and reconstituted secondary schools.

To learn more about Veronica's and Anthony's work, visit www.asiasociety.org /education.

To book Veronica Boix Mansilla or Anthony W. Jackson for professional development, contact pd@solution-tree.com.

Chapter 1

Educating for Global Competence: Redefining Learning for an Interconnected World

By Veronica Boix Mansilla and Anthony W. Jackson

This chapter draws extensively from *Educating for Global Competence: Preparing Our Youth to Engage the World* (Boix Mansilla & Jackson, 2011). Adapted with permission from the Asia Society.

Rapid economic, technological, and social changes are creating an increasingly more interconnected and interdependent world. Globalization of economies, the digital revolution, mass migration, and the prospect of climate instability are triggering new concerns and demanding a new kind of high school graduate. At the dawn of the 21st century, we are recasting our understanding of economics, communication, security, cultural identity, citizenship, and the environment. There is an increasing call for more powerful and relevant learning in response to these new demands and opportunities (Gardner, 2009; Reimers, 2009; Stewart, 2007).

To succeed in this new global age, students will need capacities that include, but go beyond, reading, mathematics, and science; they will need to be far more knowledgeable and curious about world regions and global issues, attuned to diverse perspectives, able to communicate across cultures and in other languages, and disposed to acting toward the common good. Put simply, preparing our students to participate fully in today's and tomorrow's world demands that we nurture their *global competence*, herein defined as the capacity and disposition to understand and act on issues of global significance.

Specifically, globally competent students are able to demonstrate the following four competencies.

1. **Investigating the world beyond their immediate environment**, framing significant problems, and conducting well-crafted and age-appropriate research

2. **Recognizing perspectives, others' and their own**, and articulating and explaining such perspectives thoughtfully and respectfully

3. **Communicating ideas effectively with diverse audiences**, bridging geographic, linguistic, ideological, and cultural barriers

4. **Taking action to improve conditions**, viewing themselves as players in the world and participating reflectively

Examining Global Competence

Why is global competence essential for youth in the 21st century? A broad range of forces is transforming the global landscape requiring these new capacities and dispositions. Here we examine three of the most salient.

1. The flattened global economy and changing demands of work

2. Unprecedented global migration

3. Climate instability and global environmental stewardship

These three areas of transformation illustrate a world in transition and illuminate the new educational demands that the world presents.

The rationale for global competence also rests on the value of studying the world and how it works as a potent means of engaging students deeply in learning. World cultures, transnational systems, and global issues can provide the relevance to today's world that grabs and holds students' interest. Developing global competence can thus be both a critical outcome of learning and a pathway for achieving foundational disciplinary and interdisciplinary knowledge and skills, much of which have been articulated in the Common Core State Standards (CCSS).

The Flattened Global Economy and Changing Demands of Work

Consider the changing face of the business world. A company in one country employs workers in another. Consumers in a third country buy the goods produced. Transactions involve high-speed Internet communication, the lowering of import tariffs, and government incentives for foreign investment. The result of these ordinary interconnections is a process of globalization—of unprecedented reach and breathtaking speed and consequence. *Globalization*, the accelerating traffic of goods, ideas, people, and capital around the world, has changed the face of labor (Coatsworth, 2004). Much has been written about the importance of preparing a competitive workforce able to revitalize economic growth. Understanding the changing nature of labor is critical for educators seeking to ensure economic opportunity for our youth. Perhaps most importantly, understanding changing economies in a multipolar world is critical to youth if they are to participate thoughtfully in the economies of tomorrow.

In a survey of large U.S. corporations, the Committee for Economic Development (CED, 2006), a nonprofit organization of more than two hundred business leaders and university presidents, finds that nearly 30 percent of companies believe they had failed to fully exploit their business opportunities due to insufficient personnel with international skills. Eighty percent expected their overall business to increase notably if they were to have more internationally competent employees on staff. The CED (2006) concludes:

> To compete successfully in the global marketplace, both U.S.-based multinational corporations as well as small businesses increasingly need employees with knowledge of foreign languages and cultures to market products to customers around the globe and to work effectively with foreign employees and partners in other countries.

Therefore:

> The educated American of the twenty-first century will need to be conversant with at least one language in addition to his or her native language, and knowledgeable about other countries, other cultures, and the international dimensions of issues critical to the lives of all Americans. (CED, 2006, p. 2)

Increasingly, employers are looking for competent, reliable individuals who will work at an attractive cost—regardless of location. A new distribution of labor is in the making. Computers or workers in the developing world with little training and at a very low cost are doing jobs that involve routinized tasks or scripted responses. Yet jobs that demand expert thinking and complex communication will remain in growing demand the world over. At the beginning of the 20th century, only 5 percent of the jobs in the United States required specialized knowledge and skill. By the year 2009, this increased to at least 70 percent. Workers must now be able to synthesize different types of information creatively and prepare for lifelong learning in a rapidly changing world (Gardner, 2009).

What competencies will students need to fare well in a flattened global economy? Experts have identified multiple skill sets as essential to prepare our future workforce (Levy & Murnane, 2004; Partnership for 21st Century Skills, 2009). They range from learning life long, thinking creatively, using systems thinking, and leading innovations, to exhibiting skills associated with life and careers, such as designing, evaluating, and managing one's own work for ongoing improvement and adapting to change. Collectively, they offer a dynamic portrait of learning. Surprisingly absent in public discourse about work readiness is students' lack of deep understanding around issues of global significance—how global markets operate, the promise and perils of transnational production, how social entrepreneurs contribute to human development while also meeting their bottom line, demands of economic and cultural development, and the dilemmas of inequality, to name a few.

Globally competent students prepare for a global economy by learning how to investigate matters of global significance. Are social networking technologies developing in the same ways in countries like the United States and China? What are the economic, social, and environmental consequences of outsourcing to India and Mexico? What tools do governments have to promote economic development and eradicate extreme poverty? Engaging complex and pertinent questions of this kind can encourage students to recognize their own and others' perspectives and communicate their positions clearly. Most importantly, preparing to work in a flattened global economy will require that students learn to take action. It requires that they learn to identify opportunities for productive action and develop and carry out informed plans. For example, students may learn to design and promote products to succeed in a digital world or develop an awareness campaign on the environmental consequences of their city's purchasing habits. Prepared students view themselves as informed, thoughtful, and effective workers in changing times.

Unprecedented Global Migration

International migration is happening on a larger scale than ever before, changing the demographics of classrooms and neighborhoods alike. According to data from the United Nations Department of Economic and Social Affairs Population Division (2008), in the summer of 2010, the total number of people living in countries other than those in which they were born was projected to be about 214 million. Fifty million migrants were estimated to be living in the United States. If all migrants were considered one country, it would be the fourth largest in the world in population after China (1.4 billion), India (1.2 billion), and the United States (317 million).

Migrants from the developing world bring with them ideas, know-how, practices, and skills that influence their encounters with and integration into the societies that host them. Migrants also send back home such social remittances—values, practices, and ideas that they acquire in their host country—which both promote and impede development in their countries of origin (Levitt & Lamba-Nieves, 2010). As a result, world migration is felt in the classrooms, neighborhoods, markets, and streets from both sending and receiving societies in cities like Bangalore and Buenos Aires to Boston and Brussels. Much like global markets of labor and goods, migration in the 21st century demands new educational responses. How can we best prepare youth for a world in which diversity will be the norm? How can we nurture graduates who are able to manage cultural complexity and increasingly blurred markers of origin and ethnicity? How can we prepare citizens who understand multiple spheres of participation—local, national, and global?

Whether through the media or in person, contact with individuals whose identity, culture, values, languages, and lifestyles are different will force our youth to compare others to themselves. How students make sense of this will depend on the degree to which they have been prepared to live in diverse societies. Students who have learned intercultural skills, understand multiple contexts and traditions, and have had multiple opportunities to reflect on their own worldviews in light of others' are less likely to experience difference as a threat requiring violent defense. Rather, they are more likely to experience the cultural encounter as an opportunity for exchange and collaboration (Suárez-Orozco, 2007; Süssmuth, 2007).

A growing percentage of new immigrant learners is part of a generation of transnational migrants. Unlike migrants in previous generations—and thanks to the digital revolution—these individuals are likely to remain in close contact with their countries of origin. They participate in religious, economic, cultural, and often political activity in two places. For them, healthy adaptation involves the development of a hybrid identity and dual citizenship that resists having to choose one nation over another one (Suárez-Orozco, Suárez-Orozco, & Todorova, 2008).

Schools the world over bear a new fundamental responsibility: to prepare students for difference and complexity (Suárez-Orozco, 2001, 2005; Suárez-Orozco & Sattin, 2007). They will need to prepare all youth—migrant and host alike—for new contexts in which multiple cultures coexist. Managing this complexity—fostering kinship, communicating effectively, working together, valuing difference, and benefitting from diversity—is essential to success in a global world.

What competencies will students need to fare well in a world of unprecedented migration? Preparing our youth to participate successfully in a world of increasing social, cultural, ethnic, linguistic, and religious diversity will require teaching them about the qualities—the history, languages, geography, and cultural contributions—of peoples the world over. It requires inviting them to revisit their own nation's qualities and contributions in a way that captures its multiple relations with other societies. Students should not be led to assess "how we measure up" but rather to engage in a comparative analysis that deepens understanding of a nation's historical and contemporary characteristics. Providing students with multiple opportunities to examine what happens when cultures meet—whether in their neighborhood, in their classroom, or virtually—is of the essence. The task of nurturing intercultural sophistication is not the responsibility of social studies teachers alone; it behooves art, mathematics, science, language, and second-language teachers to renew their curricula as well.

Among the capacities associated with global competence, two are at the heart of intercultural sophistication: (1) the capacity to recognize perspectives (others' and one's own) and (2) the capacity to communicate ideas effectively across diverse audiences. For example, globally competent individuals can examine and explain their own worldviews and cultural traditions, recognizing how these influence their choices and interactions in everyday life. Competent individuals can also weigh others' perspectives, considering the factors—including culture, geography, religion, and more—that inform them.

To be prepared for a world of growing cultural interaction and diversity, students will also need to understand what happens when cultures meet and influence one another. They will need to understand how differences in power, wealth, and access to knowledge affect opportunities for individuals and social groups. Thriving in a world of diversity involves communicating with diverse audiences—being able to recognize how different audiences may interpret their perspectives. It demands that students listen and communicate carefully and respectfully, using appropriate languages and technologies to do so. If recognizing perspectives and communicating with diverse audiences are at the heart of students' preparation for an interactive world, the two other competencies—investigating the world and taking action—are of no lesser value.

Students who are able to pose their own questions and investigate cultural interactions are more likely to be reflective about the complexities they present. Additionally, students who are able to envision and carry out a plan of action—perhaps to aid cultural dialogue through community service or raise awareness about different perspectives through an art exhibit or blog—come to view themselves as active contributors in an increasingly diverse world.

Climate Instability and Global Environmental Stewardship

Over the last few decades, Earth has experienced a growing frequency of extreme weather conditions and overall rising temperatures. Scientists around the world predict the prospect of further climate change is high. If greenhouse gas concentration in the atmosphere continues to rise, the consequences will be alarming and adaptation difficult. *Global warming* is too narrow a term to describe a phenomenon that is shaping life on the planet—affecting the Earth's climate, chemistry, and biology at once (Sachs, 2008). Consider a few of the consequences: ocean levels are likely to rise due to thermal expansion and the melting of polar ice sheets, affecting coastal areas and their water supply. Climate and chemistry changes are likely to impact land and sea habitats, causing large-scale extinction. Infectious diseases like malaria have already spread as rising temperatures make new regions accessible to the mosquitoes that transmit it. Rising temperatures and shifting patterns of precipitation are also affecting agricultural productivity (Sachs, 2008). An important job for the next generations will be managing the consequences of climate change and devising effective solutions for mitigation and adaptation. The challenge will be significant.

Adaptation to climate change calls for a new paradigm—one that considers a range of possible future climate conditions and associated impacts, some well outside the realm of past experience (National Research Council, 2010). Because greenhouse gases do not respect national borders, the problem is essentially a global one. Climate change is affecting every region, country, city, and village on the planet in distinct ways and shaping living conditions, job opportunities, and civic participation for youth. The search for increased energy efficiency has begun to trigger new industries and technologies—from green architecture to carbon sequestration tools. Political life the world over has seen a rise in environmental debates—in fact, the environment is a primary motivation for youth civic participation in industrialized countries (Haste, 2007). Yet despite such productive developments, a more concerted global effort will be needed to return atmospheric temperatures to sustainable levels and to adapt effectively to climate change. Mitigating and adapting to change will require furthering international climate agreements and enlisting all sectors of world societies in prudent resource use and sustainable innovation (Sachs, 2008). A comparative advantage will go to those who, based on a deep understanding of the problem, can create novel solutions. However, progress in mitigating and adapting to climate change will not stem solely from the newest technology or the latest top-level multilateral agreement. Progress will depend on the numberless private decisions of individuals who view themselves as agents of history—globally competent actors in today's world.

What competencies will students need to fare well in a world of climate instability? Preparing our students for a future of climate and environmental instability begins by helping them understand the workings of the Earth, why and how climate change (past and present) takes place, and what consequences global warming is likely to have on various habitats and ecosystems, including their own. It will require that students understand how energy consumption in one place affects living conditions of people on the other side of the world and how we all depend on the same atmosphere for life. It will require that students understand current and future climate solutions and learn to weigh their potential against their risks.

Efforts to understand climate change, its causes and consequences, will continue over the next generations, when today's youth and their children are the decision makers. Well-prepared individuals will be able to investigate climate change sources and impacts: framing local problems for study, collecting and interpreting data, and building informed arguments. Most important, these individuals will need to understand that scientific claims and projections are empirically grounded interpretations of the problem. They will need to understand that the knowledge of today may be legitimately revised when new and more compelling frameworks or evidence become available. These individuals will need to see that our understanding of climate is provisional and subject to critique—and view these qualities as markers of strength, not weakness. The global nature of climate change, paired with the multiplicity of impacts expected in various parts of the world, will demand that students learn to recognize perspectives carefully.

How does a rising ocean affect fishing populations in Alaska or in coastal tourist villages in Bangladesh and New England? How prepared is each community to face the challenge? What adaptation options do these communities have? Thinking about climate change in ways that consider multiple locations, perspectives, and concerns and communicating effectively about these various conditions prepare students for effective transnational cooperation—the kind of global approach necessary to mitigate and adapt to climate change. At a premium will be individuals who understand environmental systems around the world well. Most importantly, such individuals will find opportunities to act now as global environmental stewards preparing for the work of their generation.

In sum, educators across the globe are expected to teach core sets of concepts and skills that curriculum experts at national, regional, and local levels deem essential. Preparing youth for the work of their generation involves revisiting such core concepts and skills and putting them to the service of a deeper, better, and more participatory understanding of the world in which we live. Nurturing students' global competence enables education leaders to examine how engaging crucial global issues can catalyze learning of this core content and how learning such content can inform students' worldviews.

Defining Global Competence

Although in the 21st century the interconnectedness of our world is unprecedented, we still do not have a broadly shared definition for *global competence*.

Robert Hanvey's (1976) seminal paper "An Attainable Global Perspective" calls for education to develop *modes of thought* that include perspective consciousness, "state of the planet" awareness, cross-cultural awareness, knowledge of global dynamics, and awareness of human choices. Fernando Reimers (2009) advances the view that students need *global competency*: "The knowledge and skills that help them cross disciplinary domains to comprehend global events and respond to them effectively" (p. A29). Veronica Boix Mansilla and Howard Gardner (2007) offer a perspective on global consciousness that emphasizes "the capacity and the inclination to place our self and the people, objects and situations with which we come into contact within the broader matrix of our contemporary world" (p. 58). The International Baccalaureate Organization (IBO, 2012) cites one of its goals as developing *international mindedness*, a view of education that values the world as the broadest context for learning, develops conceptual understanding across a range of subjects, and offers opportunities to inquire, act, and reflect.

The United States is certainly not alone in recognizing the importance of preparing students to cooperate and compete in the global scene (Darling-Hammond, 2010; Kagan & Stewart, 2004a, 2004b; Stewart, 2005; Wagner, 2008). Countries around the world have seen the emergence of initiatives to infuse greater international understanding in their school curricula. For example, in a landmark document, the Maastricht Global Education Declaration, representatives of the European Council advanced a framework for global education designed to "open people's eyes and minds to the realities of the world and awaken them to bring about a world of greater justice, equity, and human rights for all" (O'Loughlin & Wegimont, 2002). In these leaders' views, global education is thought to encompass —but is not limited to—education for human rights, sustainability, peace, conflict prevention, interculturality, and citizenship (O'Loughlin & Wegimont, 2002). In Great Britain, the Department for International Development (n.d.) has sought to integrate global development issues into the formal curriculum through the Global Partnership Schools program, linking U.K. schools to schools in Africa, Asia, Latin America, and the Caribbean.

In Sweden, the Global Citizen Program prepares students, teachers, and school leaders to understand countries with significant importance to Sweden's future. Partnerships with schools in China and India are thought to prepare students for the real demands of the world, from studying abroad to engaging in sustainable development, corporate social responsibility, and economy and finances. In India, efforts toward international education build on ancient traditions of nonviolence and universal brotherhood. India's *National Curriculum Framework for School Education* calls for a school curriculum that promotes national identity and unity but also strives to "raise awareness of the necessity to promote peace and understanding between nations for the prosperity of all mankind" (Asia-Pacific Centre of Education for International Understanding [APCEIU], 2005). The framework expects international education to be embedded in existing subjects, although particular curricula focused on peace and human rights education have also been proposed (APCEIU, 2005).

The Task Force on Global Competence—a group of state education agency leaders, education scholars, and practitioners—developed the definition of *global competence* we articulated here, under the auspices of the Council of Chief State School Officers EdSteps initiative (CCSSO-EdSteps) and the Asia Society Partnership for Global Learning. This definition also framed the U.S. Department of Education's (2012) International Strategy 2012–2016. Figure 1.1 shows the framework for global competence.

What are the critical attributes of each domain of global competence? How are these competencies demonstrated in student work? In what follows, we introduce each dimension of this global competence definition, illustrating its various dimensions with exemplary units teachers around the world developed.

Investigating the World

Globally competent students ask and explore questions of critical global significance: What is the expected impact of climate change on the Gulf of Mexico or the Gulf of Guinea, Africa? How prepared are local communities to adapt to the change? How does humor differ in the United States and in Afghanistan? How has the International Criminal Court interacted with national justice systems in Kosovo and Rwanda? How do immigrant adults from different national origins experience the process of becoming American? These questions are globally significant. They address phenomena that affect a large number of people worldwide, they shed light on the diversity and commonality of experiences across localities, and they play out both in students' communities and in communities across the globe. Globally competent students can articulate the global significance of their questions and why these questions merit study.

Through careful framing and examination, important problems like these become researchable. Globally competent students do not seek a pre-established "right answer"; rather, they engage intellectually and emotionally in searching for and weighing informed responses. To do so, they identify, collect, and analyze credible information from a variety of local, national, and international sources, including sources in languages other than their own. Competent students can weigh and integrate evidence to create coherent responses and draw defensible conclusions—in writing an essay, designing a solution, proposing a scientific explanation, or creating a work of art.

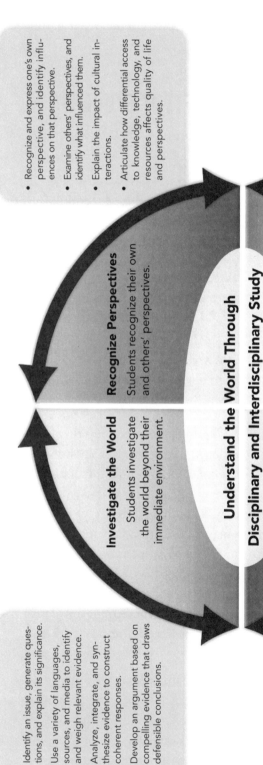

- Recognize and express one's own perspective, and identify influences on that perspective.
- Examine others' perspectives, and identify what influenced them.
- Explain the impact of cultural interactions.
- Articulate how differential access to knowledge, technology, and resources affects quality of life and perspectives.

- Recognize and express how diverse audiences perceive meaning and how that affects communication.
- Listen to and communicate effectively with diverse people.
- Select and use appropriate technology and media to communicate with diverse audiences.
- Reflect on how effective communication affects understanding and collaboration in an interdependent world.

Recognize Perspectives

Students recognize their own and others' perspectives.

Understand the World Through

Disciplinary and Interdisciplinary Study

Communicate Ideas

Students communicate their ideas effectively with diverse audiences.

Investigate the World

Students investigate the world beyond their immediate environment.

Take Action

Students translate their ideas into appropriate actions to improve conditions.

- Identify an issue, generate questions, and explain its significance.
- Use a variety of languages, sources, and media to identify and weigh relevant evidence.
- Analyze, integrate, and synthesize evidence to construct coherent responses.
- Develop an argument based on compelling evidence that draws defensible conclusions.

- Identify and create opportunities for personal or collaborative action to improve conditions.
- Assess options and plan actions based on evidence and potential for impact.
- Act personally or collaboratively in creative and ethical ways to contribute to improvement, and assess the impact of actions taken.
- Reflect on capacity to advocate for and contribute to improvement.

Figure 1.1: Framework for global competence.

Source: Reprinted with permission from Boix Mansilla & Jackson, 2011.

In the next section, we present a twelfth-grade New York student's investigation of Latin American literature. It provides an intriguing look at how investigating the world beyond local environments can manifest in student work.

GLOBALLY COMPETENT STUDENTS

Globally competent students are able to investigate the world in the following ways.

- Identifying an issue, generating a question, and explaining the significance of locally, regionally, and globally focused researchable questions

- Using a variety of languages and domestic and international sources to identify and weigh relevant evidence in addressing a globally significant researchable question

- Analyzing, integrating, and synthesizing evidence to construct coherent responses to globally significant researchable questions

- Developing an argument based on compelling evidence that considers multiple perspectives and draws defensible conclusions

Gabriel García Márquez's novel *Chronicle of a Death Foretold* explores themes of family, reputation, honor, revenge, justice, obsession, and communal responsibility. Following an in-depth study of the novel, its construction and sociocultural context, students in a twelfth-grade English language arts class at Henry Street School for International Studies, New York City, were invited to study the work of a notable Latin American poet of their choice. They had to explain the writer's global significance and examine how, as in *Chronicle of a Death Foretold*, the author's personal experience and literary choices convey his or her unique perspective. "Looking specifically at one continent of poets," the teacher explains, "enabled students to see how these storytellers not only reflect current social perspectives and cultural values, but they also have the power to direct and criticize public opinion."

One student, Janel, focused her research on José Lezama Lima, a well-regarded and debated Cuban poet. Janel characterizes this writing as complicated to understand given Lezama Lima's baroque style, which she compares to that of Luis de Góngora. In her essay, Janel demonstrates how Lezama Lima's work explores themes of disappointment, religion, sacrifice, and femininity. Accounts of the poet's life reveal how Lezama Lima's homosexuality and independent political views influenced his writing and his view of poets as interpreters of a complex and often paradoxical world. Janel explains that Lezama Lima felt alone as a child. She argues that Lezama Lima lived in a strict communist society that censored literature that might oppose the "revolutionary consciousness." Janel refers to Lezama Lima's 1966 novel, *Paradiso*, which includes detailed homosexual content for which the writer was ostracized. According to the government, Janel explains, the novel went against the Cuban Revolution in that it lacked political commitment.

To complete her depiction of context for Lezama Lima's work, Janel points out that another source of social rejection was religion, a topic about which Lezama Lima wrote extensively. Janel points out that the Roman Catholic influence on Cuban society does not approve of homosexuality, considering the writer a sinner and forcing him to sacrifice his religious beliefs. Janel concludes that, to interpret Lezama Lima's work one must understand that he felt alone in social terms and in religious terms.

Close reading of various poems, including "Melodía," enabled Janel to show how Lezama Lima's experiences were reflected in his densely symbolic work. Janel interprets this work as depicting shattered dreams—dreams that while fondly held are not permitted to become reality. Janel sees disappointment in "Melodía" as if evoking the many disappointments the author faced throughout his personal life and career. And yet, she associates the imagery of smoke to hope, to desire attained even if unconsciously. In "Melodía," Janel explains, Lezama Lima makes his readers envision solid objects in order to help them comprehend the symbolic meaning and truths that lie within the text.

How does Janel's work illustrate her capacity to investigate the world? Janel identifies Lezama Lima as an author of local and regional significance. Lezama Lima uses universal themes within the particular context of the Roman Catholic and communist society in which he grew up. As a marginalized homosexual writer, Janel explains, Lezama Lima found refuge in literature—and influenced a generation of Cuban writers.

To produce her essay, Janel must identify, interpret, and synthesize a range of sources: original and translated publications of Lezama Lima's work, biographies, and reviews produced in and outside of Latin America. Through a classical literary-analysis approach, Janel selects samples of Lezama Lima's writing to ground her argument. Through close reading, she discerns literary choices that both support and challenge her argument—that is, that marginalization plays a key role in Lezama Lima's work.

In sum, Janel draws on literary analysis tools to make sense of the work of a poet who had very different forces shaping his life than those shaping her own.

In doing so, she comes to understand the way in which this particular example of Latin American literature speaks to the political climates on which it stands.

Recognizing Perspectives

An important step students take toward global competence is recognizing that they hold a particular perspective—one that others may not share. To reach a full understanding of world issues, they must be able to articulate and explain the perspectives of other people, groups, or schools of thought. Globally competent students understand, for example, how economic conditions may inform individuals' expectations for their lives, how religion may inform people's sense of responsibility. They understand that access to knowledge and technology is unevenly distributed in the world, affecting people's views and quality of life. Deploying their knowledge of history, culture, and current events, students with global competence are able to compare their own perspectives with those of others. When needed, they can integrate these various viewpoints to synthesize a new one—the kind of comprehensive perspective vital to addressing complex global issues.

In the next section, we illustrate an example of student work stemming from a collaboration between schools in California and Bangalore, India. It provides an intriguing look at how recognizing perspectives can manifest in student work.

GLOBALLY COMPETENT STUDENTS

Globally competent students are able to recognize perspectives in the following ways.

- Recognizing and expressing their own perspective on situations, events, issues, or phenomena, and identifying the influences on that perspective

- Examining perspectives of other people, groups, or schools of thought and identifying the influences on those perspectives

- Explaining how cultural interactions influence situations, events, issues, or phenomena, including the development of knowledge

- Articulating how differential access to knowledge, technology, and resources affects quality of life and perspectives

Informed by statistics about the global rise of *mega slums* and inspired by contemporary artists' engagement with such issues, the shelter project brought together students from three educational institutions: two U.S. public schools (urban and suburban) and a learning center for the poor in a slum of Bangalore, India. Teachers Todd Elkin (Washington High School, Freemont, California), Ariel Roman (East Oakland School of the Arts, Oakland, California), and Arzu Mistry (Drishya Kalika Kendra, Bangladore, India) designed the project to raise students' awareness about global living conditions. The project encouraged students to think of themselves as contemporary artists taking part in a global conversation about how the majority of the world population lives. The teachers asked, "How does what you make as an artist relate to your responsibilities as a citizen of the world?"

The unit capitalized on the cultural, socioeconomic, and environmental diversity of the three schools, inviting students to communicate with each other and respond to each other's work through a shared blog and Skype conversations. The unit culminated with the creation of site-specific shelters. For students in the United States, the shelters represented explorations in contemporary art. For students in Bangalore, the project turned into the designs for a mobile classroom of the future—a temporary student learning space fit for meditation and study. In their designs, students were inspired to use recycled materials like colorful plastic bags and bottles to filter sunlight, creating a visually rich space for well-being. How do these students demonstrate their capacity to recognize perspectives?

For the U.S. students, the project raised awareness of world inequality and their relatively privileged lifestyles. This was especially true for suburban students, who saw in the project an opportunity to revisit their own place gratefully and critically. Students appreciated their access to technology, not having to work, and the relatively safe and tidy neighborhoods they live in. They came to understand how living in this context influences their perception of standards of living. As one student comments:

> A surprisingly high number of people live in shantytowns [and the like] and in poverty. It's funny how people tend to think that everyone lives the same way that they do, probably because we are surrounded by people with the same lifestyles. But, when you get out of your comfort zone and really see what is going on, it's crazy. We are so lucky to have what we have.

These students were also able to raise awareness and critique as contemporary artists:

> Our shelters were made for a reason. . . . They are installations that change the space. How often do you see a shantytown in the suburbs? Through all of these aspects, the shelters could create a new light around what a shelter actually is. It's not just a box.

Exchanging images and interacting online enabled students to see each other's environments and analyze differences in culture, styles, and knowledge. Todd Elkin's students at Washington High immediately noticed the learning space Arzu Mistry's students in Bangalore used—where children worked typically outdoors on the ground and barefoot. The Indian students' familiarity with natural elements and awareness of their environment became evident as they offered feedback to Elkin's students' designs. The U.S. students recognized that living and learning closer to their natural environment influenced their Indian peers' viewpoints and priorities. Ideas from the students in Bangalore established an important balance of power and respect across student groups. Consider the following examples from two of Mistry's students.

> **Nandini:** Have you thought about using your sloped roofs for rainwater collection? The edges of the roofs can have gutters on them. Look at our meditation rooms.

> **Chandrakala:** Are your homes going to have gardens? When we designed our spaces we had to think of five questions: (1) How does your space interact with the sun, wind, rain, and acoustics? (2) How do the physical aspects of the classroom inspire learning (windows, doors, boards, benches, et cetera)? (3) How does your space deal with wastes? (4) How does your space improve the environment or have a positive eco-footprint (food, forests-landscaping, wastes, electricity, other inputs . . .)? (5) How does your classroom inspire creative play? Do these five questions work for your space or models even though it's a house and not a classroom?

The collaborative nature of this project enabled students from diverse backgrounds to share ideas, influence one another's designs, and recognize similarities in approaches. Shared tasks were potent platforms for collaboration, cross-cultural analysis, and deeper understanding. One of Elkin's students, on sharing techniques for brainstorming, comments:

> I think that their poster is visually more appealing than the one that we did. It's cool to see people using the same train-of-thought method in a different part of the world. Even though I may not be able to understand what is written on the paper, the technique is relatively similar, and I think that is really neat. Articulating how differential access to knowledge, technology, and resources affects quality of life and perspectives.

Despite their drastically different socioeconomic environments, students in California and Bangalore engaged in a serious reflection about the ways in which food, shelter, and education affect people's lives. The discussion was not limited to material wealth but to the conditions that enable well-being and the individual's responsibility to consider the well-being of others. "In our opinion this unit was a sneak peek into the emotions of homeless people," comments one of Elkin's students, "but this peek is not limited to homeless people—it was a way to experience the emotions of any person who has faced [these kinds of] dilemmas in their lives." Mistry explains:

> The students were engaged in a global conversation about education for all. Heated conversations during critiques argued whether we needed to design for forty children, like in our centers, or five hundred children like in the government school next door. The children were engaged in conversations around quality, scale, and need for education. As artists they were a part of global conversations keeping their real context (socioeconomic, cultural, geographic, and environmental) in mind.

Mistry believes that reflecting about the importance of education and life experiences can help students reframe how they view their opportunities. "Most of the children we work with are children of construction workers," she explains. "We were making the leap from a field they understood and positioning them at the level of a designer with a global consciousness."

They presented their work and received feedback from architects and designers in the city, validating the importance of the work they were doing and pushing them to think beyond their concept of school and classroom. One student has continued to pursue this work and has submitted drawings and models in order to build a one-room schoolhouse in her community. Others have designed elaborate rainwater catchment systems based on research of various rainwater-harvesting models.

As this project illustrates, interaction and serious work can help students develop their beliefs about others living on opposite sides of the planet and in strikingly different socioeconomic conditions. Cross-cultural collaboration encourages them to challenge stereotypes and recognize that diversity of perspectives enriches their work—and their understanding of themselves as producers of work.

Communicating Ideas

Audiences and collaborators often differ on the basis of culture, geography, faith, ideology, wealth, and other factors. As such, globally competent students must be able to thoughtfully differentiate among audiences and adapt their behavior accordingly, working together in diverse teams toward a common goal. Because English is, at this historical moment, the world's common language for commerce and communication, globally competent students in the United States and elsewhere benefit from being proficient in English—as well as in at least one other language. Proficiency with a variety of media and new technologies is another essential component in communicating ideas globally in the 21st century.

In the next section, we illustrate an example of student work: a tenth-grade project to explore communicative tensions in colonization through contemporary art at the International School of Amsterdam. It provides an intriguing look at how communicating ideas can manifest in student work.

GLOBALLY COMPETENT STUDENTS

Globally competent students are able to communicate ideas in the following ways.

- Recognizing and expressing how diverse audiences may perceive different meanings from the same information and how that impacts communication

- Listening to and communicating effectively with diverse people, using appropriate verbal and nonverbal behavior, languages, and strategies

- Selecting and using appropriate technology and media to communicate with diverse audiences

- Reflecting on how effective communication impacts understanding and collaboration in an interdependent world

For the final project of their contemporary music, art, and theater class, tenth-grade students at the International School of Amsterdam had to create a *happening* —a fleeting artistic event or installation in the school. Their task was to explore the concept of exile in aesthetically interesting and novel ways. Students Helen, Kyoko, Noah, and Yei Jin's happening examined colonization as a metaphor for forced exile. The group chose to include the audience (teachers, researchers, and special invitees) in their piece, as they "wanted the audience to really get a sense of what colonization might feel like." They dressed in black, covered half their faces with masks, and yelled commands at their audience simultaneously in their four different native languages. Participants were unable to understand what was being said, but strong gestures indicated they were to follow the students through various stations in the happening. The students intended to elicit from their audience feelings of powerlessness and frustration, to make them feel they really were being colonized. As pressure for obedience mounted, all attempts at two-way communication broke down and the captive audience began to quietly follow the masked students. Participants were instructed to place their shawls, watches, and shoes in a box marked "Pre-Colonial History Museum" and forced to carry labels with their newly modified names.

The students' happening was in essence an examination of how communication works and makes meaning under cultural-political oppression. The students demonstrated a sophisticated understanding of how the colonized and their colonizers interpret differently their realities, behavior, and artifacts. The symbolic act of relinquishing personally meaningful everyday objects to a "museum" is just one effective strategy the students used to convey such a clash of interpretations.

The students demonstrate a capacity to integrate a range of artistic modes of expression to convey their message. "We chose masks to symbolize the difference in cultures. Once we put our masks on we were not really ourselves anymore," they note. Using a cacophony of voices and urgent, authoritarian gestures, they communicate with an audience sensitive to different forms of input. The students relate their work to that of other contemporary artists. They honor, for example, John Cage, who expanded musical expression, and Kara Walker, whose visual work examines the perverse nature of *paternalistic oppression*.

The colonialism happening illustrates the students' exquisite understanding of the role of communication in history and ethics. Their work offers a critique of ethnocentrism, the inability to listen, the failure of respect, and concomitant barriers to genuine cross-cultural cooperation. In an intelligent, reflective move, these students, hailing from different cultural backgrounds, comment on and exploit their own linguistic diversity to advance a common aesthetic goal. Engaging in a rich examination of communication—its limits, pitfalls, and potential for abuse—raises students' awareness of the responsibilities associated with verbal and nonverbal expression in engaging others, near or far.

Taking Action

Globally competent students do more than collect knowledge about the world—they seek to make a difference in the world. Furthermore, they do not postpone their contributions for when they grow up (Fischman, Solomon, Greenspan, & Gardner, 2004). Rather, they see and create opportunities to act today—in their neighborhood or on the global stage. Alone or in collaboration, ethically and creatively, globally competent students envision and weigh options for action based on evidence and insight. They can assess the potential impact of their plans, taking into account varied perspectives and potential consequences for others. Lastly, they demonstrate courage—in acting and in reflecting on their actions.

In the next section, we turn to an example of student work to examine the challenges and opportunities students encounter when taking action: a fourth-grade British student's essay on the children of political refugees, which received a young journalist award. It provides an intriguing look at how taking action can manifest in student work.

GLOBALLY COMPETENT STUDENTS

Globally competent students are able to take action in the following ways.

- Identifying and creating opportunities for personal or collaborative action to address situations, events, issues, or phenomena in ways that improve conditions

- Assessing options and planning actions based on evidence and the potential for impact, taking into account previous approaches, varied perspectives, and potential consequences

- Acting, personally or collaboratively, in creative and ethical ways to contribute to improvement locally, regionally, or globally, and assessing the impact of the actions taken

- Reflecting on their capacity to advocate for and contribute to improvement locally

Florence Potkins is eleven years old—a fourth-grade student at Drayton Park Primary School in London. She has a strong interest in World War II, which the books of such writers as Morris Gleitzman and Michael Morpurgo, as well as the diary of Anne Frank, have triggered. When she learned about an Amnesty International and *The Guardian* competition calling for a report on human rights, she remembered a conversation she had recently had at home. Florence and her parents were talking about human rights, and the conversation turned to the topic of detention centers in the United Kingdom. A study that she read had recently shown the harmful and long-lasting psychological and physical impacts on the children of refugees forced into detention centers. Prompted by her desire to raise awareness about the issue, Florence began conducting her own research. Her findings are captured in her essay "Is This Nazi Germany?" which won the upper primary category of Amnesty International's Young Human Rights Reporter of the Year 2010 (Drabble, 2010).

In her essay, Florence describes the plight of an eleven-year-old girl, Bethlehem Abate, and her mother who awoke one night as "dark men in uniforms" ransacked their home, despite their cries, before forcing the mother and child into a dark vehicle. They did not know where they were being taken or how long they would be there.

Bethlehem and her mother were taken to Yarl's Wood, a detention center in Bedfordshire for asylum seekers where each year 1,000 children are taken in. The pair had earlier escaped to England from Ethiopia where Bethlehem had been abused by her father. If Bethlehem were to be forced to return to Ethiopia, she would be taken from her mother, an Eritrean woman, and be alone with no one to take care of her. Her mother would suffer a worse fate—being taken into custody or killed.

Florence writes that, to Bethlehem, going to Yarl's Wood was "like going to prison for an awful crime." Bethlehem's story does not sound like something that could happen in England, but it did. As Florence astutely noted in her essay, "This is not Nazi Germany; this is September 2009 in Leeds" (Drabble, 2010).

Reading about children's experiences in detention centers disturbed Florence: "I was so worried to learn about so many children that were in detention centers and had no proper education, no proper childhood." Florence's parents and teachers encouraged her, and she decided the essay contest was a good opportunity to write about the topic. She explains, "Before we talked about it, I had no idea that human rights violations were happening in England. Before we talked I always thought that human rights violations were things that happened in India or Africa, and I had no idea they were happening here. It was horrible."

In her view, the essay would help "raise awareness about children in detention centers. No child should suffer this appalling lack of education and lack of freedom." Florence decided that focusing on a girl about her age would be an effective narrative technique, highlighting the contrast between her safe and comfortable life and that of her subject. Florence's essay seeks to build on the tradition of girls from the past she admires, like Anne Frank.

The recognition for her essay led Florence to think about doing even more for the sake of refugee children. She joined a young campaigners' group at Amnesty International working to increase public awareness in the United Kingdom, where the government is deciding to abolish child detention, granting children of refugees legal status upon arrival. Florence adds:

> I am really hoping that I can make a difference. Many campaigners are working to make detention centers better. I understand that we may have to have detention centers but you don't have to call them such horrible names, you don't have to torture people there—not physical torture but psychological torture. You don't have to put them through such a horrible and very destructive experience that has a big impact on people's lives . . . leaving them scarred for life.

Asked whether she, as a child, can indeed make a difference, Florence replies with hope that she can contribute to the work many others are doing. Grateful for all the support she has received, she understands the key role her family plays and those teachers who encouraged her to voice her opinion. She enjoys the feeling of having found a cause that matters to her: abolishing child detention and knowing that "whatever happens, you stood up for something you believed in."

Conclusion

Virtually every major issue people face—from climate change to national security to public health—has a global dimension. Information technologies ensure that news from every country reverberates around the world in minutes. With over two hundred million migrants worldwide, migration and immigration are creating magnificently more diverse neighborhoods, communities, and nations. More than ever, people, cultures, and nations are interdependent, requiring the preparation of students capable and disposed to solve problems on a global scale and participate effectively in a global economic and civic environment. No longer a luxury for a few, global competence is a requirement for all.

Reflecting a variety of subject-specific and interdisciplinary scenarios, the student work featured in this chapter demonstrates that global competence can be developed across ages, disciplines, and educational institutions. The task at hand is to move global competence from the margins to the mainstream of education and cultural policy—in the United States and beyond. One thing is clear: the magnitude and significance of this enterprise demand that educators take actions—small and large, individual and collective—to make global competence a priority in policy and practice.

References and Resources

Asia-Pacific Centre of Education for International Understanding. (2005). Education for international understanding in India: Appraisal and future perspectives. *Journal of Education for International Understanding, 1*, 49–66.

Boix Mansilla, V. B., & Jackson, A. (2011). *Educating for global competence: Preparing our youth to engage the world.* New York: Asia Society.

Coatsworth, J. H. (2004). Globalization, growth, and welfare in history. In M. M. Suárez-Orozco & D. Qin-Hilliard (Eds.), *Globalization: Culture and education in the new millennium* (pp. 38–55). Berkeley: University of California Press.

Committee for Economic Development. (2006). *Education for global leadership: The importance of international studies and foreign language education for U.S. economic and national security.* Accessed at http://ced.issuelab.org/resource/education_for _global_leadership_the_importance_of_international_studies_and_foreign _language_education_for_us_economic_and_national_security on October 31, 2012.

Darling-Hammond, L. (2010). *The flat world and education: How America's commitment to equity will determine our future.* New York: Teachers College Press.

Department for International Development. (n.d.). *Global schools partnership.* Accessed at www.dfid.gov.uk/Documents/funding/global%20schools/pil-section1.pdf on April 30, 2010.

Drabble, E. (2010, May 31). The winners of the Young Human Rights Reporter of the Year competition. *The Guardian.* Accessed at www.theguardian.com/education/2010 /jun/01/human-rights-amnesty-competition-winners on October 2, 2013.

Fischman, W., Solomon, B., Greenspan, D., & Gardner, H. (2004). *Making good: How young people cope with moral dilemmas at work.* Cambridge: Harvard University Press.

Friedman, T. L. (2007). *The world is flat: A brief history of the twenty-first century* (Rev. ed.). New York: Farrar, Straus & Giroux.

Gardner, H. (2004). *How education changes: Considerations of history, science, and values.* Accessed at http://old-pz.gse.harvard.edu/PIs/HowEducationChanges.pdf on May 13, 2013.

Gardner, H. (2009). *Five minds for the future.* Boston: Harvard Business School Press.

Hanvey, R. G. (1976). *An attainable global perspective.* New York: American Forum for Global Education. Accessed at www.globaled.org/an_att_glob_persp_04_11_29 .pdf on May 13, 2013.

Haste, H. (2007). Good thinking: The creative and competent mind. In A. Craft, H. Gardner, & G. Claxton (Eds.), *Creativity, wisdom, and trusteeship: Exploring the role of education* (pp. 96–104). Thousand Oaks, CA: Corwin Press.

International Baccalaureate Organization. (2012). *IB answers*: *What is international mindedness?* Accessed at https://ibanswers.ibo.org/app/answers/detail/a_id/3341 /~/what-is-international-mindedness%3F on October 24, 2012.

Kagan, S. L., & Stewart, V. (2004a). International education in the schools: The state of the field. *Phi Delta Kappan, 86*(3), 229–241.

Kagan, S. L., & Stewart, V. (2004b). Putting the world into world-class education: Introduction. *Phi Delta Kappan, 86*(3), 195–196.

Levitt, P., & Lamba-Nieves, D. (2010). *"It's not just about the economy, stupid"—Social remittances revisited.* Accessed at www.migrationinformation.org/Feature/display .cfm?id=783 on April 30, 2010.

Levy, F., & Murnane, R. (2004). *The new division of labor: How computers are creating the next job market.* New York: SAGE.

Mansilla, V. B., & Gardner, H. (2007). From teaching globalization to nurturing global consciousness. In M. M. Suárez-Orozco (Ed.), *Learning in the global era*: *International perspectives on globalization and education* (pp. 47–66). Berkeley: University of California Press.

Márquez, G., & Rabassa, G. (2003). *Chronicle of a death foretold: A novel.* New York: Vintage International.

National Research Council. (2010). *Adapting to the impacts of climate change.* Washington, DC: National Academies Press. Accessed at http://dels.nas.edu /resources/static-assets/materials-based-on-reports/reports-in-brief/Adapting _Report_Brief_final.pdf on April 30, 2010.

O'Loughlin, E., & Wegimont, L. (Eds.). (2002). *Global education in Europe to 2015: Strategy, policies, and perspectives.* Accessed at www.coe.int/t/dg4/nscentre/Resources /Publications/GE_Maastricht_Nov2002.pdf on March 19, 2013.

Partnership for 21st Century Skills. (2009). *P21 framework definitions.* Accessed at www.p21.org/documents/P21_Framework_Definitions.pdf on April 30, 2010.

Reimers, F. (2006). Citizenship, identity and education: Examining the public purposes of schools in an age of globalization. *Prospects, 36*(3), 275–294.

Reimers, F. (2009). "Global competency" is imperative for global success. *Chronicle of Higher Education, 55*(21), A29.

Reimers, F. (2010). Educating for global competency. In J. E. Cohen & M. B. Malin (Eds.), *International perspectives on the goals of universal basic and secondary education* (pp. 183–202). New York: Routledge.

Sachs, J. D. (2008). *Common wealth: Economics for a crowded planet.* New York: Penguin Press.

Stewart, V. (2005). A world transformed: How other countries are preparing students for the interconnected world of the 21st century. *Phi Delta Kappan, 87*(3), 229–232.

Stewart, V. (2007). Becoming citizens of the world. *Educational Leadership, 64*(7), 8–14.

Suárez-Orozco, M. M. (2001). Globalization, immigration, and education: The research agenda. *Harvard Educational Review, 71*(3), 345–365.

Suárez-Orozco, M. M. (2005). Rethinking education in the global era. *Phi Delta Kappan, 87*(3), 209–212.

Suárez-Orozco, M. M. (2007). *Learning in the global era: International perspectives on globalization and education.* Berkeley: University of California Press.

Suárez-Orozco, M. M., & Qin-Hilliard, D. B. (Eds.). (2004). *Globalization: Culture and education in the new millennium.* Berkeley: University of California Press.

Suárez-Orozco, M. M., & Sattin, C. (2007). Wanted: Global citizens. *Educational Leadership, 64*(7), 58–62.

Suárez-Orozco, C., Suárez-Orozco, M. M., & Todorova, I. (2008). *Learning a new land: Immigrant students in American society.* Cambridge: Belknap Press of Harvard University Press.

Süssmuth, R. (2007). On the need for teaching intercultural skills: Challenges for education in a globalizing world. In M. M. Suárez-Orozco (Ed.), *Learning in a global era: International perspectives on globalization and education* (pp. 195–212). Berkeley: University of California Press.

United Nations Department of Economic and Social Affairs Population Division. (2008). *International migrant stock: The 2008 revision.* Accessed at http://esa .un.org/migration/index.asp?panel=1 on April 30, 2010.

U.S. Department of Education. (2012). *Succeeding globally through international education and engagement: U.S. Department of Education International Strategy 2012–16.* Accessed at www2.ed.gov/about/inits/ed/internationaled/international -strategy-2012–16.pdf on November 19, 2012.

Wagner, T. (2008). *The global achievement gap: Why even our best schools don't teach the new survival skills our children need—and what we can do about it.* New York: Basic Books.

 **Silvia Rosenthal Tolisano, MS,** is a Curriculum 21 faculty member who specializes in upgrading curriculum content to include skills and literacies of the 21st century. She has worked as a computer teacher, web designer, world language teacher, technology integration facilitator, and 21st century learning specialist.

Silvia's passions include globally connected learning, information visualizations, technology integration, and 21st century skills and literacies, as well as digital storytelling. She is known internationally in the edublogosphere and Twittersphere as *Langwitches*. Her website Langwitches (www.langwitches.org) shares examples from classrooms around the world, helping educators break down the steps in updating the traditional lesson process to make it more in line with the 21st century. Her ability to represent ideas visually and design resources has gained her tens of thousands of readers and followers from all over the world.

She holds a bachelor's degree in Spanish with a minor in international studies and a master's in education with an emphasis in instructional technology. She was born in Germany and raised in Argentina. She lived many years in the United States and currently resides in Brazil.

To learn more about Silvia and her work and engage in a learning conversation, visit her blog at www.langwitches.org/blog and follow her on Twitter @langwitches.

To book Silvia Rosenthal Tolisano for professional development, contact pd @solution-tree.com.

Chapter 2

The Globally Connected Educator: Talking to the World— Not Just About the World

By Silvia Rosenthal Tolisano

Global awareness was placed in my cradle, as the German saying goes. I was born in Germany to a mother who had lived abroad in England in the early 1960s and a father who spent the first twenty years of his life in South America. My family satisfied its *fernweh* (German for the ache one feels for distant places, the strong desire or craving to travel abroad) by taking off to other countries during every spare moment. Finally, when I was a teenager, my parents moved us across the Atlantic to Argentina; from there, I later immigrated to the United States. Time zones, airports, traveling, other languages, and other cultures were always a part of my world.

Communicating with letters, photographs, and by telephone with distant friends and relatives sprinkled across various continents was necessary but intermittent. Passing information between countries was often painfully slow, difficult, and sometimes impossible. Radio, newspapers, and television often ignored much of the news from distant places that were close to our hearts and of interest. Technology had not yet caught up with our reality. We needed to connect with people beyond our physical vicinity, but the geographic distances created too great a barrier to the other languages, cultures, and perspectives we craved.

The term *global* has almost become a buzzword and not only in education. Daily, we hear about the global economy, global warming, global citizens, global issues, global knowledge economy, globalization, global curriculum, global skills, and global competencies. Is it a fad, a trend in education? Will the global interconnectedness of our current lives go away?

Becoming a Globally Connected Educator

In the past, educators maintained professional connections with colleagues in their building and through infrequent professional development opportunities, conferences, or university courses; they might have been passive or active members of various electronic mailing lists or participants in discussion forums. How do these locally isolated educators move toward becoming globally connected teachers? The process of moving from a traditionally isolated professional in a classroom with closed doors to a connected, networked member of a global learning community is achieved in small steps. This chapter is divided into five sections to reflect those steps, which are designed to inform, guide, and coach educators from awareness to global connectedness:

1. Raising your awareness

2. Making a commitment

3. Developing your competence with contemporary tools

4. Building your personal learning network

5. Amplifying your curriculum

The goal for the connected educator is to achieve a degree of fluency that goes beyond digital literacy. Christian Briggs, coauthor of *Digital Fluency: Building Success in the Digital Age* (Briggs & Makice, 2012), explains the difference between digital literacy and digital fluency in his blog *SociaLens*:

> Note that a literate person is perfectly capable of using the tools. They know how to use them and what to do with them, but the outcome is less likely to match their intention. It is not until that person reaches a level of fluency, however, that they are comfortable with when to use the tools to achieve the desired outcome, and even why the tools they are using are likely to have the desired outcome at all. (Briggs, 2011)

Fluency thins classroom walls by allowing collaboration with colleagues, experts, and peers from around the world.

Raising Your Awareness

Since the turn of the millennium, instant access to technology and the Internet has increased dramatically, along with the availability and affordability of tools. Smartphones and tablets and tools such as Twitter, YouTube, Skype, Flickr, Blogger, and WordPress are just some ways we can connect with the world. What has not increased at the same rate, however, is the awareness that most educators have about the tools and their potential to increase global literacy. For educators to become fluent in using tools that encourage professional development on a global scale and that support their own global connectedness, they first need to become aware of the possibilities and the opportunities for global learning.

How do we become aware of learning opportunities to support global literacy? We all need to ask ourselves—as Vicki Davis, a high school teacher and cofounder of the Flat Classroom Project from Camilla, Georgia, has—how do we not only read about, watch, and learn about the world but also "learn to talk to and work with the world" (V. Davis, personal communication, December 12, 2011)?

The Definition of Global Literacy

You may think of the term *global literacy* as a measurement of the literacy levels of adults around the world. The National Center for Education Statistics (n.d.) defines *literacy* as the "ability to use printed and written information to function in society, to achieve one's goals, and to develop one's knowledge and potential." For the purpose of this chapter, *global literacy* is an individual's ability to understand global education and competencies, while being able to switch fluently between local and global perspectives. Furthermore, global literacy is the ability to access, cultivate, and maintain a worldwide network of peers and experts.

The Council of Chief State School Officers EdSteps Project, in partnership with the Asia Society Partnership for Global Learning, defines *global competence* as "the knowledge, skills, and dispositions to understand and act creatively and innovatively on issues of global significance" (Council of Chief State School Officers, 2010). Veronica Boix Mansilla and Anthony W. Jackson (2011), in their book *Educating for Global Competence: Preparing Our Youth to Engage the World,* identify four competencies for global competence: (1) investigate the world, (2) recognize perspectives, (3) communicate ideas, and (4) take action. (Refer to chapter 1, page 5, for a more detailed examination of these competencies.) In addition to defining global competence, the authors also tell us *why* global education is imperative:

Teaching and assessing student work that addresses issues of global significance around the world or in students' own backyards are essential to a world-class education system. The global marketplace is real, and today's schools must prepare students to participate, interact, and thrive in it. The more our students know about recognizing the challenges and opportunities of an interconnected world, the better they will be able to work in it and improve it. Our students' well-being, the vitality of our communities, and the welfare of our nation depend on it. (Boix Mansilla & Jackson, 2011)

The Case for a Globally Connected Educator

In his book *The World Is Flat*, Thomas Friedman (2007) tells us that globalization is unlikely to go away. Friedman shares the advice he had for his own children: "The world is being flattened. I didn't start it and you can't stop it, except at a great cost to human development and your own future" (p. 571).

As educators, we wonder, what will our students' future hold in terms of working on global teams, and how will we keep up by becoming globally competent enough to prepare our students for their nascent world? It is not only our students' future that should concern us in regard to globalization but also our own future as professionals and learners.

Heidi Hayes Jacobs (2010) opens her book *Curriculum 21* with the question, "What year are you preparing your students for? 1973? 1995?" (p. 1). We are charged with preparing our students to become competent in information, networking, media, global literacy, and digital citizenship—referred to as new literacies—as well as traditional literacy in reading and writing.

Can we, as educators, afford to see no relevance in global connections for our students? Can we realistically be satisfied with believing that global connections should be confined to the social studies classroom in elementary school and a geography course or foreign language class here and there in middle and high schools? Should mathematics, science, or English language arts classes not embed global thinking as part of their learning environments?

Awareness Strategies

The skills and literacies of the 21st century should not be one particular subject, class, or project; the critical skills of global connectedness, communication, and collaboration need to become part of the fabric of all learning—no matter what the subject area. The following list provides strategies for raising your awareness of global issues—for understanding that we are not alone in this world and that there is an abundance of material available to increase your and your students' global literacy.

- **Gain a global perspective:** Listen to, watch, read, and stay informed about global news and issues on television, radio, newspapers, and the Internet.

- **Read authors from countries other than your own:** Subscribe to blogs, such as *Book Around the World* (http://bookaroundtheworld.blogspot.com) and *Around the World in 80 Books* (http://aroundtheworldin80books .wordpress.com), to find inspiration, recommendations, and reviews of books set in different countries.

- **Read books about global topics:** Include books in your reading list that inform you about global projects like *Flattening Classrooms, Engaging Minds* (Lindsay & Davis, 2012), global thinking like *The Global Achievement Gap* (Wagner, 2010), global education like *Global Education: Using Technology to Bring the World to Your Students* (Peters, 2009), and *Growing Up Global* (Tavangar, 2011).

- **Start a conversation:** Make the effort to contact and engage with people who speak other languages, celebrate different traditions, and hold culturally different points of view than your own. Speak with a colleague who already has participated in global projects.

- **Watch a television show with a global perspective:** Choose a show filmed in or about a distant place—such as *The Amazing Race* (CBS, 2001–present) or *Around the World in 80 Plates* (Bravo, 2012–present)— to become aware of other cultures, traditions, and customs.

- **Watch a foreign film:** Learn about differences in ways of life and points of view through stories. For example, watch *The Best Exotic Marigold Hotel* (2012; England, India), *Slumdog Millionaire* (2008; India), *The Official Story* (1985; Argentina), *Almanya* (2011; Germany, Turkey), *Honey for Oshun* (2011; Cuba), *Cherry Blossoms* (2008; Germany, Japan), *For My Father* (2007; Israel), *Outsourced* (2006; India), *Good Bye, Lenin!* (2003; Germany), *Love in the Time of Cholera* (2007; Colombia), *The Motorcycle Diaries* (2004; Argentina, Chile, Peru, Bolivia), or *Whale Rider* (2002; New Zealand).

Making a Commitment

After raising awareness, the next step is making a commitment to learning how to become globally connected. The commitment goes beyond merely *seeing* the importance to making it a priority in professional development and curriculum connections. The notion of being globally connected expands from meeting once, twice, or three times a year with like-minded educators at professional workshops or conferences to daily short infusions of global connectedness with colleagues beyond your local area. Take the four competencies for globally competent students (see page 6) of investigating the world, recognizing perspectives, communicating ideas, and taking action; apply them to yourself as an educator; and even extend them to a commitment for your entire school community.

The following strategies will help you embed global awareness, interconnectedness, news, and education regularly and naturally into your learning habits, rather than making them one-time or infrequent occurrences.

- **Regularly read news in foreign languages to gain a global perspective:** Use an online translator if necessary; subscribe via an RSS reader (for example, Feedly or Flipboard) to organize and stay up to date on global issues in a personalized and regular manner.

- **Participate in globally oriented conferences to connect with and learn from like-minded educators:** These could be physical conferences that involve travel and meeting other participants face to face, or they could be virtual, where you participate by watching or listening to presenters via asynchronous video, audio presentations, or live synchronous webinars.

- **Share your own globally connected experiences as a learner and a teacher:** Strategically participate in globally oriented online or physical platforms by blogging, tweeting, collaborating on a wiki, or actively joining and contributing to a Google Group.

- **Use a variety of tools, platforms, and instructional methods:** Access these tools during your own learning in order to connect and bring the world to your students. An educator who has experienced professional learning through engaging interaction and communication with colleagues is more likely to be able to translate the process of learning for his or her students. Likewise, a teacher who learns with and from colleagues an ocean away is more likely to connect and expose his or her own students to a similar experience.

- **Model global connections and collaboration:** Be a transparent connected learner by inviting your students to be a part of your online presence and making your thinking and learning visible to them.

- **Provide small, regular infusions of global connectedness:** Rather than giving students a once-a-year, large global project that runs parallel to your curriculum, infuse global connections as a part of everyday learning. For example, traditionally, you might have used a global project, such as communicating with pen pals for a letter exchange; asked your students to create a travel brochure or poster about a faraway country; or made time to have students present current events to the class. Rather than giving students such a project, infuse global connections as a part of everyday learning. Choose to collaborate with students from other countries, cultures, and with different perspectives on a wiki to research, collect, and organize information that will shed light onto the subject you are studying from different angles. Regularly read and comment on blogs from classrooms around the world. Connect to other classrooms from around the world via Twitter to hear about students' daily lives, their questions, and what they are learning.

Developing Your Competence With Contemporary Tools

Once educators raise their awareness and make a commitment to global competencies, they can extend their learning to contemporary tools that encourage and support connection and collaboration with the world. Educators could find themselves handicapped if they lack the skills to use tools that facilitate global connections. Because they are free or low-cost, I have chosen Skype, Twitter, Google Apps, and wikis as a starter kit for globally connected educators who are looking to fill their toolbox. Digging deeper into these tools—developing true competence beyond mere technical know-how—allows educators to thoroughly examine their pedagogical use.

- **Skype** is a video-conferencing tool for class-to-class communication in real time. Skype allows for meetings, presentations, or workshops between people in different locations. With one Internet-connected computer, smartphone, or tablet with a camera, microphone, and speakers, a teacher and his or her class can work with others who are far away.

- **Twitter** is a social network microblogging platform. It is an invaluable tool for global connections. Informally, as a lurker (a person who reads but does not contribute), you can start following other educators' tweets—comments written in 140 characters or less. Take advantage of freely shared advice, links to resources, ideas, and conversations around education. By registering as a member, you can use Twitter as a marketplace to find collaborative partners by answering someone else's call or by sending out your own search for the right connection for you and your students. With Twitter, educators can receive tidbits of news in real time from around the world.

- **Google Apps** (www.google.com/enterprise/apps/education) is another family of tools that globally collaborating educators are using to organize, plan, poll, share, document, and crowdsource. *Crowdsourcing* is "an online, distributed problem-solving and production model" (Brabham, 2008). Google Apps allows users to work together to access and edit common documents, spreadsheets, forms, and presentations. When collaborators are working far away from each other, Google Apps is handy and more efficient than merely exchanging emails. Partners in a collaborative project can create a global crowd by inviting others to contribute to a document, sharing the workload by adding points of view, resources, and experiences.

- **A wiki** is a website developed collaboratively by a community of users, allowing any user to add and edit content. Wikis are particularly well-suited for educators and students collaborating on a global scale. Wikis allow the relatively easy creation of an information hub with multiple editors to include text, video, images, and so on. One of the most famous examples of global collaboration is Wikipedia (www.wikipedia.org). Wikipedia is built on a wiki platform. By using a wiki service, such as Wikispaces (www.wikispaces.com/content/teacher), collaborators have the ability to design a website infrastructure to connect, embed, and hyperlink different sections of their collaboration.

Building Your Personal Learning Network

Once you have acquired a basic capacity to use strategic tools, you are ready to move on to building a global personal learning network (PLN) that will connect you to global projects that you can join or help you promote your own globally connected activities. In their book *Personal Learning Networks*, Will Richardson and Rob Mancabelli (2011) define a PLN as:

> The rich set of connections each of us can make to people in both our online and offline worlds who can help us with our learning pursuits. While we've always had those types of people in our day-to-day lives, the Internet pushes the potential scope and scale of those networks to unprecedented heights. (p. 21)

To be globally connected, you must surround yourself with a network of globally connected, like-minded spirits. You can build this network in two ways.

1. **Join a pre-established group:** By joining, you will reap the benefits of a group of teachers who are on the same page as you and are ready, willing,

and able to work collaboratively across geographic boundaries and time zones. Then build your global network by adding connections from interactions in these established projects. These new connections become part of your PLN and are potential future collaborative partners when you strike out with your very own original project.

2. **Facilitate your own project or activity:** When you create your own group, you can tailor the goals to your vision and your students' needs for global awareness, communication, collaboration, and fluency without adhering to the structure someone else put into place.

You can already see that connecting, collaborating, and communicating with other educators who are on a mission to become globally connected for themselves and for their students creates professional relationships and trust with many individuals. Opportunities for impromptu teaching will arise when teachers make connections to specific geographic areas, with subject-area experts, or about unexpected perspectives that will lead to organic learning moments.

Let's look at three examples of how teachers took initiative to create their own globally connected project. A fifth-grade teacher from the United States (originally from Denmark), Pernille Ripp, had an idea of connecting her students to the world and created the Global Read Aloud project. She describes her motivation as follows:

> I founded the project because I believe books are powerful. Books, by themselves, spellbind people, particularly children, and allow them to travel to new places. Books become such a personal experience that to take a book and have children listen to it around the world at the same time, could open up the world. They would understand that the experience they were having with the book was perhaps the same experience as another child in another place was having. My students understand through this project that they are part of something bigger, that other kids were just like them even if they were so far apart. Even if the sun didn't rise at the same time or the seasons were opposite, they were the same because they loved the same book. (Ripp, n.d.)

Michael Graffin, an educator from Australia, decided to connect educators from around the world to discuss issues about the global classroom. He hoped to create a community of educators who answered yes to the following questions:

> Do you enjoy meeting teachers around the world? Are you interested in global education and/or global collaboration? Have you

heard about global projects, but don't know where to start? Are you interested in flattening your classroom walls? Are you on Twitter? (Graffin, n.d.)

Chrissy Hellyer, a teacher in Thailand who is originally from New Zealand, decided to take matters into her own hands when the International Dot Day, inspired by the book *The Dot* by Peter Reynolds (2004) approached in 2012. The International Dot Day seeks to inspire children and adults from around the world to connect their creativity and to "make a mark" (Reynolds, 2004). Hellyer published a call for participants on her blog, *Teaching Sagittarian*, explaining the project and giving step-by-step directions about how to participate (Hellyer, 2012).

Getting started in building a global personal learning network is relatively easy when joining already established projects; someone else took the time to conceptualize the idea, develop, and organize the project. However, it takes time, focus, and commitment to incorporate a global network into your daily professional and classroom learning. The following strategies are some examples of ways to incorporate a global network into your classroom.

Student Blogging Challenge

If you have a classroom blog, or if your students write their own blogs, you could participate in the Student Blogging Challenge (http://studentchallenge .edublogs.org), a ten-week challenge allowing students to connect with a global audience. Twice a year (March and September), Sue Wyatt, Sue Waters, and Ronnie Burt coordinate the challenge, and thousands of classrooms and students participate. Your class would automatically have other students from around the world to connect with and an audience reading and commenting on its writing. The challenge outlines the projects (ten weekly tasks), so as an educator, you can concentrate on supporting your students in producing quality writing using a blogging platform and connect your curriculum objectives to mini-lessons. The tasks range from developing a thoughtful "about me" page, learning to create avatars, using hyperlinks as part of digital writing, inserting images and media while observing copyright laws, to connecting to other participants' blogs and leaving quality comments. As students choose from a variety of activities to complete these weekly tasks, the teacher is able to connect the content to their subject-area standards and goals. A language arts teacher might ask her students to write a persuasive essay as one of the blog-writing activities. A math teacher might request a screencasting tutorial designed by his students to share various methods of solving an equation.

Teddy Bears Around the World

For younger students, Teddy Bears Around the World (www.langwitches.org/blog/travel/teddybearsaroundtheworld) is an interesting project. As a class, students write from the perspective of their teddy bears about daily life, traditions, and customs from their particular location in the world. By joining the project, students read about other countries, gain global awareness, and interact by receiving and leaving comments for other participating teddy bears.

Flat Classroom® Projects

Cofounders Vicki Davis and Julie Lindsay designed the Flat Classroom Project (www.flatclassroomproject.net), which "is a global collaborative project that joins together middle and high school students. . . . The topics studied and discussed are real-world scenarios based on the book *The World Is Flat* by Thomas Friedman" (Lindsay & Davis, n.d.).

Davis and Lindsay have created a well-designed and organized platform that supports teachers in connecting their students globally by going beyond mere contact with peers from other countries and cultures to truly allowing them to work and problem solve together.

> One of the main goals of the project is to "flatten" or lower the classroom walls so that instead of each class working isolated and alone, 2 or more classes are joined virtually to become one large classroom. The project is designed to develop cultural understanding, skills with Web 2.0 and other software, experience in global collaboration and online learning, awareness of what it means to live and work in a flat world, while researching and discussing the ideas developed in Friedman's book. (Lindsay & Davis, n.d.)

Video Conferencing

Another option is to use video conferencing to make connections around the world and facilitate collaborative work beyond reading and writing. Once you have access to and are familiar with a video-conferencing tool, such as Skype or Google Hangouts, you and your students can speak to the world. It's important to be careful and not just invite *anyone* into your classroom, so it is a great idea to join a pre-established community or network of video-conferencing educators, such as Around the World With 80 Schools (www.aroundtheworldwith80schools.net) or Skype in the Classroom (https://education.skype.com). These project hubs allow teachers to find like-minded colleagues capable and willing to use video conferencing as a way to bring authentic voices into the classroom. Connecting with another class via Skype could take on the form of a quick, one-time, five- to ten-minute call to exchange hellos and collect data, such as local weather conditions, favorite books, or cultural traditions. It could also become a venue to regularly connect classes to collaboratively work on problem solving, gather or analyze research, or receive unique perspectives to gain deeper understanding of global issues.

Twitter Network

As previously noted, Twitter is a social networking tool that allows educators to easily connect on a global level. Let's look at specific applications for teachers using this platform to build their learning networks. Hundreds of thousands of educators from around the world are connecting and communicating with each other in 140 characters or less. Connecting with, talking to, and collaborating with colleagues in other countries or continents and across oceans and time zones can become as commonplace as speaking to your colleagues in the same building. The samples of Twitter posts that follow showcase dissemination, connections, participation, and collaboration aimed at opening the classroom walls.

Mark Engstrom shared with another educator and his PLN about a collaborative global project he was involved in:

> That's exactly what we do. Your stud could (for e.g.) collaborate with students from Israel, Jordan, and Sweden. It's awesome! (@markengstrom, 2013)

I use Twitter frequently to reach out to my PLN in order to connect my students to potential subject- or content-area experts or to receive authentic data or feedback. For example:

> Kindergarten Kids want2know HOW u get 2work (transportation)& where u live.PLEASE fill out the form for them&RT (@langwitches, 2013a)

> MiddleSchool students 2become Tutorial Designers. Looking 4"experts"2give authentic advice&feedback in design process (@langwitches, 2013b)

When you become part of a Twitter network, you connect with educators worldwide, read about their projects, and participate in chats with other globally minded educators. Start out by following a few established global educators, such as Linda Yollis (@lindayollis), Kim Cofino (@mscofino), Edna Sackson

(@whatedsaid), Michael Graffin (@mgraffin), Chrissy Hellyer (@nzchrissy), Maggie Hos-McGrane (@MumbaiMaggie), Cristina Milos (@surreallyno), Julie Lindsay (@julielindsay), Vicki Davis (@coolcatteacher), or myself (@langwitches). In addition, take a look at the people they follow on Twitter. Also, pay attention to the educators they are communicating and collaborating with, and choose to follow some of them.

Twitter also has the option of creating lists of members, categorized by specific topics. Find a globally connected educators' list such as my list of international educators (https://twitter.com/#!/langwitches/international-educators). Pay attention to their Twitter profiles and read their latest tweets to see if your areas of interest match and you feel that they would be valuable contributing members of your learning network.

Further Resources to Explore

There are many websites dedicated to the globally connected educator. Sometimes we might even get inundated with too many resources. Finding a trusted organization, individual, network, or hub to filter these resources and opportunities for you becomes a necessity. Curriculum 21 maintains such a site on the Global Partnership Hub (www.c21hub.com/globalpartnership). Heidi Hayes Jacobs and I curate global projects, news, sample web 2.0 tools, and links to support each one of the four global competencies (see page 6; CCSSO, 2010; Boix Mansilla & Jackson, 2011). The site also offers a global curriculum menu (www.c21hub.com /globalpartnership/global-curriculum-menu) for strategic decisions in global curriculum design. The menu will help educators make discerning choices that will assist their students in becoming globally competent in the 21st century. Other resources include the Asia Society, Discovery Education's Global Education Partnership, and Think Global, the Development Education Association.

Amplifying Your Curriculum

The fifth and final step in becoming a globally connected educator is amplifying your curriculum. *Amplification* means to enlarge or to extend. The power of learning is amplified with the help of tools that bring the world into your classroom. In the past, amplification might have meant finding authentic opportunities for learning, such as bringing guest speakers into the classroom—colleagues, acquaintances, family, or friends of friends. These amplifications extended the curriculum by including real-life primary sources of information and lifting learning off the pages of the textbook. Before technological advancement, teachers read books, spoke with colleagues, went to workshops, or continued

their education at the university level to further their own professional learning. In 21st century classrooms, amplification brings learning from beyond the
local. The world is at our fingertips. Geographic constraints and the limits of
a local professional network have fallen away. Yong Zhao (2010), in the article "Preparing Globally Competent Teachers: A New Imperative for Teacher
Education," talks about this "death of distance" (p. 422). The opportunities
to communicate, collaborate, and learn with people from around the globe are
endless. No longer do we have to rely on local options only. If a teacher has one
Internet-enabled device, she is ready to establish a global communication hub
for herself and her students.

Amplification happens when students no longer work only in collaborative
teams with peers who are sitting next to them in the same classroom. Their
peers are citizens of the world, at home in different continents, in different time
zones, and with different mother tongues. Amplification happens when students
go beyond writing an essay "for the refrigerator [door]," as David Jakes (2007)
comments on the blog post "Rationale for Educational Blogging" (Davis, 2007).
Students write for a global audience, not just for their teacher or parents. As Alan
November (2013) advocates, "An audience of one, the teacher, is no longer suffi-
cient to prepare students for success in the global economy."

Students experience the potential of thousands or more people looking at their
work, giving them feedback, and understanding that their work is authentic and
meaningful. Amplification means doing work for more than a letter grade: it
means acknowledging that our work is part of a global whole.

How does amplification in the classroom happen when a globally connected
educator facilitates the learning? Let's look at several examples of subject-
specific strategies.

Geography

A middle school class is studying South America and following, via a blog and
Twitter feed, a National Geographic–sponsored trip of a man traveling by bus
from the United States to Antarctica. Students learn about the traveler's different
destinations throughout South America: Mexico, Guatemala, the Panama Canal,
Colombia, Argentina, and finally, Cape Horn, Chile, his last bus stop before setting sail across the Drake Passage for Antarctica (http://travel.nationalgeographic
.com/travel/bus-to-antarctica/trip-essay-traveler). Their teacher then contacts the
traveler via Twitter. The students take their learning beyond the pages of a book,
or a screen for that matter, by video conferencing using Skype with the traveler
and talking with him about his adventures.

In another example, each student chooses one newspaper article a week to present to his or her classmates. The teacher uses the news to connect to the geography curriculum. Amplification happens when the teacher upgrades the assignment by partnering with a class from another country to collaboratively contribute to a Google Map. Every week, students mark the geographic location of their current event articles on the map. They create a title, summarize the content of the article in 140 characters or less, categorize the news into political, environmental, entertainment, and so on, and link back to the original news source. After a few weeks of adding placemarks, they have created a map that provides an incredible visual and becomes a medium to further explore geography, information literacy, and global awareness. Questions such as these arise: In what categories do most news events we added fall? In what continents and countries are the news events from? What area of the world do we know or hear the least about? Why? How can we expand our horizon to cover more areas of the globe? Are we interested in different news events due to our geographic location? Does geographic location influence perspectives? Further amplification happens when the students make the map public and invite people living in the areas of the news events to comment.

Mathematics

Students create tutorials of mathematics problems to teach classmates difficult concepts or to provide struggling students with extra help. To amplify the activity, their teacher contacts a mathematics teacher from another country through her Twitter network to give her students the opportunity to collaborate on these tutorials and receive feedback. The two teachers create a wiki as a platform and coach students as they build a site structure, organize, categorize, and then embed the tutorials, which are designed in different media (video, audio, and so on). Students compare and contrast different methods of solving problems (caused by different teaching methods and traditions).

English Language Arts

An elementary school student writes a book report, creates a movie trailer for the book, and then embeds it on his blog. The author of the book contacts the student, offering to arrange a Skype conference with the entire class to discuss her work. With this activity, the teacher amplifies the learning by connecting the curriculum to the outside world.

A middle school student writes an essay about Jewish war veterans, in particular about one soldier who was killed in the Iraq war. The essay, published on the classroom blog, catches the attention of the fallen soldier's family and friends who contact the teacher to express their gratitude for honoring their son, brother, and friend. Amplification happens when students realize that they are not writing for an audience of one—their teacher—or just to receive a grade; rather, their writing can make a difference in other people's lives. They are digital citizens with an online footprint.

A class of fourth graders in the United States connects with three other classes spread over other continents in an intense quad-blogging month. Each week, one team writes blog posts while the other teams comment on them. The following week, the roles rotate. Amplification happens when students examine the wave of comments from peers in other countries. Their work goes beyond their writing to take them to other geographic locales, time zones, cultures, and ways of life.

First-grade students work on a creative writing assignment based on the imaginary travels of Flat Stanley, a character based on the book *Flat Stanley* by Jeff Brown (2006). Students research their chosen destinations and write about the imaginary travels of their "flat self." They incorporate local landmarks, weather conditions, and the sights and sounds they might encounter.

From the writing activity evolves a collaborative script for a podcast of the Flat Stanleys, which students then produce and then place on the class blog. One student, Jasmine, sends her imaginary Flat Jasmine to London, England. A blog reader and podcast listener from England writes encouraging comments on the class blog about how well Jasmine described her city. As the Flat Stanleys "travel" to new destinations, other students from around the globe make connections by leaving comments for the emerging readers and writers. The activity gives students an opportunity to measure how far their voices traveled. The class tracks the locations on Google Earth and measures the distances between their hometown and the location of those who comment. Amplification happens when students' writing does not just stay in a paper journal that the teacher grades but when students record their writing as a podcast episode to share on the classroom blog.

Social Studies

Fifth-grade students go beyond the textbook to learn about Christopher Columbus. They create a survey to collect their own data on global perspectives about this historic figure. Was Christopher Columbus a hero, victim, or villain? How many adults still remember facts they learned about him when they were in fifth grade? Amplification happens when the students disseminate the survey on their classroom blog and via Twitter to collect over four hundred responses from around the world within a few days. Students analyze the data from the survey to learn about how perspectives differ based on geographic location. Students interview a Native American via email and a teacher from South America via Skype to learn about their unique perspectives about Columbus. They Skype with students from China to compare Chinese explorers during the time of Columbus. In addition, they communicate with a class from the Ukraine to investigate if and what its textbook teaches about Christopher Columbus.

As elementary students learn about the American Revolution, their teacher connects them to a high school teacher via Skype to discuss the battles of the revolution. They also connect via Skype to an author and descendent of a Revolutionary War soldier to hear personal stories about his ancestor. They use Twitter with mentors from England (other educators) to discover a different historical perspective of the same events. Amplification happens when students tap people—rather than just a textbook—for information, specifically people in different geographic locations who have different points of view, experiences, and expertise.

Arts

An art class learns about the artist Pablo Picasso. Amplification happens when the U.S. teacher connects with an art teacher from Madrid, Spain. The teachers collaborate to design a lesson plan that involves each teacher facilitating a lesson via Skype to the students from the other class. As students learn about the artist and share their research, students in Spain take a field trip to the Museo Nacional Centro de Arte Reina Sofía. They take videos, capture images, and record themselves as they view Pablo Picasso's work and learn about him and then exchange their learning virtually with their partner class. Teachers digitize students' artwork that is based on Picasso's work. Once the artwork is in digital form, the classes piece together the individual files to form a mosaic and post it on their classroom sites.

Physical Education

An entire school participates in International Sports Day, where students compete in track-and-field events against their peers. Amplification happens when the school connects with other schools from around the world, and each team uploads their times and scores to a collaborative wiki or by filling out a Google Form alongside the other participating schools. Students analyze the collected data and interpret the results of the global competition.

Students create videos of unique (not widely known) games from their country or region. They simply film the game, without offering any explanation. Amplification happens when students embed their videos on a collaborative wiki so that participating classes from around the world can view the videos and attempt to figure out the rules of the game. For example, children from Germany might share a video of them playing völkerball, while children from New Zealand record a game of netball. Additionally, students might record a video of a typical playing field or venue for a popular game or sport, such as soccer, basketball, or swimming. Students then compare and contrast sports venues throughout the world. For example, they might examine how a soccer field looks in the middle of New York City versus in the suburbs of Sydney, Australia.

World Languages

Students in one classroom field-test an iPad app for creating a game. Their task is to design an interactive game for younger students to review foreign language vocabulary. Amplification happens when, after creating the game, students review the app on their blogs, including suggestions about how to improve it. Their teacher tweets and blogs about the students' work, linking to their reviews. The app developers become aware of the reviews, and the next app update includes one of the student's suggested changes. Activities such as this show students that they can have an impact. Learning to document, write, and share on a platform accessible to the world allows the students to become part of a conversation; their opinions matter and have value.

Conclusion

Global interconnectedness should not be a goal for the faraway future. Global networking and collaboration are real, right here and now, and doable for educators and students. Tools that help facilitate these connections and collaborations are now abundant and free to any user with an Internet-capable device. To be globally connected, schools need globally competent administrators and teachers, and a globally oriented curriculum. Global education must go beyond the once-in-a-school-year project—schools must embed international activities into *all* learning. Classrooms have to embed foreign language study, exposure to global issues and perspectives, and global collaboration early on and continuously as part of the learning culture.

The five steps outlined in this chapter support a strategic shift in the way we learn and who we learn with as professionals. Becoming fluent in a globally connected world requires immersion—listening, speaking, writing, and communicating with those in other cultures.

For the connected educator, global fluency is the ability to move effortlessly between local and global connections for his or her own ongoing professional development and for the benefit of his or her students. It means collaborating with colleagues and students we might never meet face to face, who live on other continents and across time zones, from another culture, maybe in another language. It means calling on experts, eyewitnesses, or volunteers at a moment's notice—that a teachable moment in your classroom prompts. Global fluency also means taking research and primary sources off the pages of a book and connecting students to firsthand knowledge or different points of view than their research from a local library might provide.

Fluency means bringing in perspectives beyond the local news—maintaining a growing worldwide PLN that serves as a discussion board, generates ideas, and provides potential collaborative partners. It includes the ability to choose appropriate tools for specific tasks, such as video conferencing, wikis, backchannels, and synchronous and asynchronous communication without feeling paralyzed when unforeseen situations arise, and they will!

Global fluency means to move confidently as a learner, participant, and producer using global social networking, curating, and blogging platforms. Administrators model for their faculty what it means to be a connected learner. They take learning beyond the text of a professional journal or book by bringing in experts virtually to share multiple points of view from their global learning network. Educators become part of a global research team examining best practices. They connect their faculty and students to an amplified way of learning by documenting, sharing, and disseminating information. Professional development opportunities in globally connected schools also shift from isolated training sessions for specific software tools or lectures about methods to globally connected, ongoing, anytime, anywhere, and anyhow learning opportunities that foster collaboration and relationships between educators around the world.

References and Resources

Boix Mansilla, V. B., & Jackson, A. (2011). *Educating for global competence: Preparing our youth to engage the world*. New York: Asia Society.

Brabham, D. C. (2008). Crowdsourcing as a model for problem solving: An introduction and cases. *Convergence: The International Journal of Research Into New Media Technologies, 14*(1), 75. Accessed at http://con.sagepub.com /content/14/1/75.abstract on March 16, 2013.

Briggs, C. (2011, February 5). The difference between digital literacy and digital fluency [Web log post]. Accessed at www.socialens.com/blog/2011/02/05/the-difference -between-digital-literacy-and-digital-fluency on February 2, 2013.

Briggs, C., & Makice, K. (2012). *Digital fluency: Building success in a digital age*. New York: SocialLens.

Brown, J. (2006). *Flat Stanley.* New York: HarperCollins.

Council of Chief State School Officers. (2010). *EdSteps: Collecting work samples for global competence.* Accessed at http://edsteps.org/CCSSO/SampleWorks /GlobalCompetence.pdf on October 20, 2012.

David Jakes. (2007, January 17). Re: Rationale for educational blogging. Accessed at http://anne.teachesme.com/2007/01/17/rationale-for-educational-blogging on June 20, 2013.

Davis, A. (2007, January 17). Rationale for educational blogging [Web log post]. Accessed at http://anne.teachesme.com/2007/01/17/rationale-for-educational -blogging on October 29, 2012.

EdSteps. (n.d.). *Global competence.* Accessed at www.edsteps.org/ccsso/Manage Content.aspx?system_name=I5nka44NofDD3IY38QBonx%20Crwfdw%20uF on October 26, 2012.

Friedman, T. L. (2007). *The world is flat: A brief history of the twenty-first century* (Rev. ed.). New York: Farrar, Straus & Giroux.

GfK Roper Public Affairs. (2006). *Final report: National Geographic—Roper Public Affairs 2006 geographic literacy study.* Accessed at www.nationalgeographic.com /roper2006/pdf/FINALReport2006GeogLitsurvey.pdf on October 20, 2012.

Graffin, M. (n.d.). *The global classroom chats.* Accessed at http://theglobalclassroom chats.wikispaces.com on October 26, 2012.

Hellyer, C. (2012). *Dots around the world collaborative project.* Accessed at http://teachingsagittarian.com/2012/09/dots-around-the-world-collaborative -project on October 20, 2012.

Jacobs, H. H. (Ed.). (2010). *Curriculum 21: Essential education for a changing world.* Alexandria, VA: Association for Supervision and Curriculum Development.

Lindsay, J., & Davis, V. A. (n.d.). *Flat classroom.* Accessed at www.flatclassroom project.net/about.html on August 19, 2013.

Lindsay, J., & Davis, V. A. (2012). *Flattening classrooms, engaging minds: Move to global collaboration one step at a time.* Boston: Pearson.

Langwitches. (2013a, August 18). MiddleSchool students 2become Tutorial Designers. Looking 4"experts"2give authentic advice&feedback in design process http://langwitches.org/blog/2013/08/18/11-toolkit-class-re-design [Tweet].

Langwitches. (2013b, May 17). Kindergarten Kids want2know HOW u get 2work(transportation)& where u live.PLEASE fill out the form for them&RT https://docs.google.com/spreadsheet/viewform?formkey=dGJWM3lHVEdPYVBl MzhKR2NmamNZTHc6MQ#gid=0 [Tweet].

Mansilla, B., & Jackson, A. (2011.). *Educating for global competence: Preparing our youth to engage the world*. Accessed at www.edsteps.org/CCSSO/Sample Works/ EducatingforGlobalCompetence.pdf on August 20, 2013.

markaengstrom. (2013, August 13). @payanar That's exactly what we do. Your stud could (for e.g.) collaborate with students from Israel, Jordan, and Sweden. It's awesome! [Tweet].

National Center for Education Statistics. (n.d.). *Definition of literacy*. Accessed at http://nces.ed.gov/naal/fr_definition.asp on October 25, 2012.

November, A. (2012). *Who owns the learning? Preparing students for success in the digital age*. Bloomington, IN: Solution Tree Press.

November, A. (2013). *Education workshops for educators*. Accessed at http://novemberlearning.com/professional-development-services/education -workshops-for-educators on March 16, 2013.

Peters, L. (2009). *Global education: Using technology to bring the world to your students*. Washington, DC: International Society for Technology in Education.

Pollock, D. C., & Reken, R. E. V. (2009). *Third culture kids: Growing up among worlds*. Boston: Brealey.

Reynolds, P. (2004). *The dot*. Cambridge, MA: Candlewick Press.

Richardson, W., & Mancabelli, R. (2011). *Personal learning networks: Using the power of connections to transform education*. Bloomington, IN: Solution Tree Press.

Ripp, P. (n.d.). The global read aloud [Web log post]. Accessed at www.globalread aloud.com on October 30, 2012.

Tavangar, H. S. (2011). *Growing up global: Raising children to be at home in the world*. New York: Ballantine.

Wagner, T. (2010). *The global achievement gap*. New York: Basic Books.

Zhao, Y. (2010). *Preparing globally competent teachers: A new imperative for teacher education*. Thousand Oaks, CA: SAGE. Accessed at http://jte.sagepub.com /content/61/5/422.full.pdf+html on October 30, 2012.

William Kist, PhD, is an associate professor at Kent State University. A former middle school and high school language arts teacher, Bill has also served as a language arts and social studies curriculum coordinator and as a consultant and trainer for school districts across the United States, specializing in technology integration and curriculum mapping.

Bill has been researching classroom uses of new media across disciplines and grade levels since the late 1990s. He has presented in the United States and internationally and has over fifty articles and book chapters to his credit. His profiles of teachers who are broadening our conception of literacy are included in his books *New Literacies in Action: Teaching and Learning in Multiple Media* (2005) and *The Socially Networked Classroom: Teaching in the New Media Age* (2010). Building on this work, *The Global School: Connecting Classrooms and Students Around the World* (2013) describes teachers who are using new media to collaborate with students and teachers across the world.

While serving as director of the Commission on Media for the National Council of Teachers of English (NCTE), he also had the opportunity to be lead coeditor for NCTE's Pathways for 21st Century Literacies, an online professional development curriculum focusing on new literacies. Bill continues to be sought out for interviews in the press regarding new literacies, including such publications as *U.S. News & World Report* and *Education Week*. A member of the National Book Critics Circle, he reviews books for Cleveland's *The Plain Dealer* and remains active as a filmmaker and musician, having earned a regional Emmy nomination for outstanding music composition. Throughout his career as an educator, Bill has remained active as a professional musician. His original music has been compiled on his album *Movie Music*.

To learn more about Bill, visit his blog at www.williamkist.com or follow him on Twitter @williamkist.

To book William Kist for professional development, contact pd@solution-tree.com.

Chapter 3
Taking the Global and Making It Local: A Qualitative Study

By William Kist

In September 2011, I was fortunate to be present in a kindergarten class in a small rural district in Ohio on a day when iPads were being given out to the students. Each kindergartener would receive a tablet computer to use not only in class but at home as well. The iPads were stored on large carts, and the students knew immediately what was about to happen as the carts were wheeled into each classroom. The teachers had spent several days working with both students and parents on the proper uses of the tablets. The students were barely able to contain themselves as they knelt on the carpet waiting for the teacher to call their names.

Each student marched up when his or her turn came, taking the iPad in hand in a fashion reminiscent of a senior in high school receiving his or her diploma. Then, each student returned to his or her place, gazing at the iPad and waiting for direction. In some cases, the students couldn't contain themselves and started to use their iPads, opening apps that were familiar to them. Teachers were not too strict at this point, not wanting to ruin the moment. Once teachers passed out all the iPads, they began the process of integrating them into their classrooms.

Of course, when I heard about this kindergarten iPad project, one of the first questions I asked the district's stakeholders was, "Why? Why are you giving kindergarteners iPads?" The answer I received from the superintendent was loud and clear: "To help our students compete on an international stage." This wasn't the answer I expected from the superintendent of a small school district located in a county with a large Amish population. The idea of globalism as the prime motivator behind the project hadn't occurred to me as I was dodging horse and buggies on the road to the school.

Yet this superintendent was convinced that giving five-year-olds iPads to use through their elementary years was necessary to position the students of this small community to be competitive globally. She felt students needed to be competitive because, as she talked to community leaders, many of them were involved in businesses that either exported products or collaborated on international projects. At the very least, she and the community leaders felt that their local students could be left behind by a world that is transitioning to a new way of reading, writing, and communicating.

When I spent some time in the kindergarten classrooms of this district during the 2011–2012 school year, I didn't see much use of the iPads explicitly for global education. There were some apps that had obvious applications for global education, such as The Weather Channel, WeatherBug, and the Montessori Approach to Geography. Using these apps, the students could check the weather all over the world and look at maps of other countries, for example. However, most of the time I was in the classrooms, students were using the iPads for making words or basic number functions. Students would be directed to open the Magnetic Alphabet app, which resembles just what it implies—the magnetic letters that kids like to manipulate on a refrigerator or other metal device. The teacher would write a word such as *cat* on the whiteboard at the front of the room and then direct students to make a new word from the same word family by taking the *c* off of the front of the word and substituting another consonant.

When I brought up the fact that not much instructional time was devoted to clearly international issues, the answer I got from the teachers was that simply interfacing with the iPad was positioning students to become part of an international community. Just knowing what an app is and how to use one helps level the playing field, as millions of people across the world use similar interfaces on their tablets or phones.

It was very clear that the students understood the basics of how to use their iPads, even on the first day they received them. Students seemed to adapt very quickly and often helped their teachers. Students were also very conversant with terminology such as *app* and *updating*. When they saw the instructional technology administrator enter the room, they would ask, "Are our apps being updated today?" Throughout the year, the teachers noticed how often students helped them understand the iPad interface. "It's easy for them to figure out how to play these apps," commented one teacher. Both teachers and students seemed to feel that the machines were user-friendly. There were some logistical issues related to the storing and charging of the iPads and the syncing up of the apps across classrooms, but teachers and students seemed to grasp navigating on the iPads themselves. The only complaint I heard was related to problems playing videos and that Apple doesn't allow Flash.

Although technology sometimes gets criticized for driving us apart as human beings, I actually saw many instances in which students were helping each other (and their teachers) with their iPads. It was a common occurrence to see students, usually in pairs, laughing and talking about something they were looking at on an iPad screen. If anything, it was the teacher who seemed to always be dragging the students back from collaborative work and the students who wanted to help each other and share their successes. These students seemed poised to be able to collaborate with anyone in the world who had an iPad, iPhone, iPad Mini, or any other similar device.

Exploring the Flat World

As Thomas Friedman (2007) and many others express, we live in a flat world, meaning that while some of the world is still closed off, for the most part, our world is increasingly open to us to explore, if not in person, then via the Internet. The increasingly internationalized world we live in is not only impacting the creative worlds, such as music and fashion, but also our politics and our economies as well. It is probably no coincidence that the Common Core State Standards (National Governors Association Center for Best Practices & Council of Chief State School Officers [NGA & CCSSO], 2010) put great emphasis on preparing students to be global citizens. Many college readiness reports that highlight the need for middle and high school students to be prepared to succeed in an internationalized job market support this goal (International Baccalaureate, 2012; National Council for the Social Studies, 2010; Partnership for 21st Century Skills, 2011). Often, however, these curriculum standards identify the need to be global without really being specific on exactly what skills students need to adequately navigate the world (at least via the web). What skills do students need for global education?

Many teachers and scholars are advocating for a broadened, global conception of literacy in this age of international new media. This chapter summarizes research I've done since 2000 documenting several collaborations between U.S. teachers and teachers in other countries. This research has been published in the book *The Global School* (Kist, 2013). These collaborations took several different forms with the data revealing several salient themes: how this broadened global conception of literacy served to compare and contrast common life experiences with those of students in various countries; how the ongoing dialogue between the teachers in different countries served to unpack instructional practices prevalent both in the United States and the country being studied, serving to critically examine classroom discourse; and how the teachers had to work to surmount obstacles to achieve the international collaborations.

The ultimate purpose of this chapter is to report on the work of teachers who are attempting to operationalize this call for more global education. What does a truly global classroom look like at the K–12 level, and what have these pioneering teachers had to overcome to effect these international collaborations? This work is part of a long-term research project to describe the work of innovative teachers who are attempting to integrate new media into their daily classroom practices (Kist, 2005, 2010, 2013).

As the Internet became a part of our daily lives and the theoretical work of early scholars influenced educators (New London Group, 1996), teachers and students from across the globe have attempted to figure out the practical, daily implications of creating a screen-based rather than a page-based classroom. Since the late 1990s, I have attempted to capture and profile their work, almost as a film documentarian would, trying to describe the very real challenges and triumphs that these pioneering teachers have experienced.

As humans have grappled with learning the new literacies, some theoreticians have focused on the social practices and events associated with literacy in general, and this has formed the core of what has become known as the New Literacy Studies. Colin Lankshear and Michele Knobel (2003) define the new literacy studies as referring to "a specific sociocultural approach to understanding and researching literacy" (p. 16). If we are to look at literacy as inextricably linked to social context, then linked to that focus may be criticism of the power structure in that social context, as well as its prevailing discourses (Fairclough, 1989, 1995). As Rebecca Rogers (2002) defines this perspective, "Critical literacy concerns itself with disrupting dominant social practices through resistant reading and writing of texts" (p. 773). Those who write from a critical literacy perspective suggest that we need to uncover these power dynamics in texts for kids and that all voices in our classrooms need to be heard, regardless of preference of medium (Delpit, 1995; Freire, 1970; McLaren, 1989; Morrell, 2002; Willinsky, 1990).

Adding a global element to the critical literacy lens has been a natural fit for many of these enterprising teachers who have attempted to create classrooms without walls. What has guided much of the work of these teachers is a kind of intercultural critical literacy (Myers & Eberfors, 2010), a perspective suggesting using new media to open up a dialogue between classrooms with a goal of engendering a form of critical literacy that crosses boundaries. This intercultural critical literacy thrust may or may not be aligned with the goals and objectives of the Common Core, leading to some interesting tensions for classroom teachers and students alike.

The focus of this chapter on global education has been part of a lengthy qualitative study that has involved analyzing interview transcripts as well as sample assignments and rubrics that teachers across the world have created. Eleven teachers are the focus of the international part of the study, including four outside of the United States. A fuller description of the work of these teachers and their involvement in using social networking to further global education is included in my book *The Global School* (Kist, 2013). What follows are brief descriptions of trends in the data.

Overcoming Barriers With Simple Projects

Many teachers are interested in internationalizing their classrooms, but even those who are interested in relatively simple projects report barriers and obstacles. A common barrier is the school itself, as many districts block some websites—such as Twitter, Facebook, and even Google—preventing students from using them to aid in collaboration. Of course, these barriers are in place for a reason: security concerns. These fears may be a major reason why the social networking aspects of web 2.0 haven't made their way into 21st century classrooms and why they remain mainly afterschool activities (Kist, 2010). The unregulated web 2.0 world is frightening to educators and many stakeholders.

In the face of these barriers, some teachers interviewed for this study chose less-complicated international projects. For example, teachers asked students to create their own international field trips. Students could accomplish such a project in the pre-Internet days, and it could, of course, still work with 21st century students. The goal of the assignment is to get students to construct an itinerary—like a TripTik that the local automobile club might furnish. Students could plot out historical places to visit for social studies class, for example. Or they could construct a science field trip that takes students to see key natural phenomena. The Internet makes such projects possible—even in 3-D as students take virtual tours, such as through the Smithsonian National Museum of Natural History (www.mnh.si.edu/panoramas) or the Grand Canyon (www.nps.gov/grca/photos multimedia/virtualtour.htm).

Foreign language teachers have long used celebratory immersion projects to help students understand the cultures of the foreign languages they study, and these kinds of experiences take very little technology. Students studying Spanish, for example, may bring in food related to the holiday Cinco de Mayo. On the day of the celebration, teachers may ask students to bring in movies or music of the country they study. Using technology to build on this kind of immersion project, some foreign language teachers use online speaker avatars such as those created through such sites as Voki. Teachers have the ability, for example, to create an avatar of themselves speaking a foreign language and asking questions that the students must answer also using the foreign language. Teachers may construct dialogues around such familiar scenarios as ordering food at a restaurant or going to the doctor.

Another relatively basic assignment that supports web 2.0 is to assign students to read preselected international blogs related to the topic of study. Students are expected to read and perhaps leave comments before reflecting on what they've read. Such an assignment may be relatively easy for the teacher to set up, in that he or she can identify a set number of websites that the school technology director can unblock. For example, if the teacher is doing a unit on a specific country, he or she could preselect certain blogs from that country. Perhaps one blog could focus on the food of a specific country, while another focuses on tourism, and so on. The students' assignment is simply to visit and read a certain number of these preselected blogs per week and, if possible, leave a comment on one or more of the blogs. Another related assignment would be for students to provide a summary of what they have learned by visiting the various international blogs. Thus, internationalizing of the curriculum occurs, exposing students to unfiltered voices from other countries, without violating school rules.

Another relatively simple international collaboration is to assign students to read news accounts described in various news sources. Many foreign newspapers have online English versions, such as English Pravda (http://english.pravda.ru) or Le Monde in English (https://twitter.com/LeMondeInEN). Apart from assigning students to focus on just one news event, the teacher can ask students to look at the top headlines from each online newspaper and compare them to the top headlines from U.S. newspapers. Just having a conversation about what items are newsworthy in foreign countries compared with what gets the most ink at home is an activity that broadens the horizons of U.S. students. The standards of journalism in place (or not) in foreign countries compared with U.S. news outlets may surprise students as well.

Teachers can also assign students to read books or view films from other countries. These are simple assignments that any teacher with a well-stocked local or school library can confidently create. Assigning students to read books, view films, or eat food of another country are all low-tech ways for teachers to expose students to international ideas and global cultures. As mentioned, foreign language educators have often done these kinds of projects to help open their students to the culture they are studying. Now, teachers of all subjects are attempting these kinds of projects, as the need to globalize instruction cuts across many disciplines.

Reaching Out

For districts that have slightly less-strict Internet safety policies, teachers are asking their students to interview or make contact in some way with international figures. The student may be required to interview an international expert in some area via email or Skype, for example, or perhaps just make contact with a librarian, professor, or teacher in pursuit of answers to questions the teacher provides. This expert could be from a local university or one across the world. The point is that the students are getting to connect with experts on international issues. A slightly more complicated project involves students following Internet scavenger hunts that may include pinpointing the workplace of an expert to interview. In one example, students use Google Earth to find various places of interest related to a historical character they are studying, or they assemble artifacts, either real or virtual, related to a certain culture they are studying. There are several sites, such as Google Lit Trips, that feature premade scavenger hunts that any student can take with a computer and Internet access. Teachers could use such hunts as models for students to create their own scavenger hunts. Teachers interviewed for this study reported combining the virtual scavenger hunts with real scavenger hunts in which students follow clues posted in various places in the school to find items or accumulate objects related to a foreign country or international culture.

Other teachers have modified the old-fashioned pen-pal assignment, requiring students to maintain regular communication with an international student via letters or email. Various websites exist that help teachers match up their students with international pen pals. Teachers can assign students to ask certain questions or focus on certain topics during interactions with their pen pals. Teachers can easily convert these conversations into ongoing collaborations. Some teachers require students to interview local community members who may have a tie to an international community, and this local person may suggest one or more friends or family members still living in the international country who may be willing to correspond with the student.

Collaborating Internationally

The goal of many teachers who use the Internet to globalize classrooms seems to be arranging for collaboration among students in classrooms spread throughout the world. There seem to be several trends of these kinds of classroom projects. Teachers tend, first of all, to have students in their respective classrooms read common texts. Students in the collaborating countries may read a core text. Teachers then set up a traditional literature circle with students taking turns facilitating the discussion as they move through the text together. In pursuit of the goal of an intercultural literacy, many teachers choose a core text that illuminates some central question students are studying. Other teachers have created text sets (Kist, 2005; Short & Harste, 1996) juxtaposing a variety of texts to explore an international theme. Students can assemble text sets themselves that are multimodal—putting together lists of novels, graphic novels, films, and visual art (to name a few forms of representation) from their respective countries that deal with topics of study.

Frequently, teachers provide students in these kinds of collaborative projects with some type of platform to enable them to communicate with each other. Sometimes this takes the form of a wiki, which teachers may set up and fill with student work. Teachers use such sites as Wikispaces or PBworks to set up wikis with pages that invited students in collaborating classrooms can access. The wikis may be set up in such a way that only the invited students can edit the pages, but anyone in the world may view the pages. This has the benefit of allowing students to have an international audience as they are building the wiki pages. Essentially, the wiki becomes a huge research paper, filled with not only words but also links to videos, music, PowerPoints, and whatever documents students find that illuminate the topic they are studying and writing about.

The advantage of using a wiki is that teachers can organize it in such a way that groups of students can collaborate on various pages, loading those pages with all kinds of multimodal links. If two classes are collaborating on a wiki focusing on characteristics of cities, for example, one wiki page could concentrate on public transportation while another page could focus on volunteer opportunities. Each group would include students from several different classrooms who would collaborate on filling that page with as much relevant material as possible, forming their own Wikipedia on whatever topic or essential skill they are studying.

Some projects, such as the Flat Classroom Project, require collaborative groups to work together to produce a video, or some other kind of multimedia text, with some group members providing footage while others provide parts of the script or music or storyboarding. Another pre-existing collaborative project that teachers may tap into is the World Savvy Challenge (http://worldsavvy .org/youth-engagement/world-savvy-challenge) in which teams work together to solve problems. Additionally, students can take part in such projects as Amnesty International's Write #4Rights (www.amnestyusa.org/writeathon). There are many such projects available for teachers who don't want to create their own collaborative projects.

Understanding Benefits and Challenges

Teachers who are involved in these international projects are generally pleased with the depth of the conversation occurring between their students. Teachers noted the synergy that occurs when students from very different cultures work together on a common project. A common rationale expressed for working on these kinds of collaborative projects is that students will need, quite possibly, to work with international colleagues as part of their careers. As businesses continue to outsource and sell products on an international level, students who have worked on global education projects in school will, supposedly, have an advantage over those students who have not.

Teachers also reported certain challenges related to international collaborations. Several mentioned wrestling with how much to keep students on task as they communicate with students overseas. Of course, this kind of dilemma could be seen as similar to off-task behaviors that teachers must deal with in face-to-face environments. Most teachers in the global collaboration projects felt in the end that some amount of off-task chatter was acceptable and even desirable as students got to know each other. In the end, off-task conversation may help further the goals of the global education projects in that students may learn more about other cultures through such informal conversations.

Teachers also wished they had more professional development to help them get ready for these kinds of projects. Even the newest teachers, who are supposedly *digital natives* (Prensky, 2005), may be baffled about the plethora of new communication tools available and how to make the best use of them in the classroom. In recent years, I have been teaching future teachers who were born after 1990, and I've found that they have expressed some of the same ambiguity about new media as earlier generations, such as the baby boomers, might express. Some typical comments were, "I feel like I wouldn't really use very much new literacies [in teaching], because I don't know how they will affect the students" and "I agree with not being a fan of the iPad or Kindle. . . . I love to flip the pages and smell that new book smell." We can't automatically assume that younger teachers have a higher comfort level with new media than older teachers do.

Setting up an international collaboration is not easy. There are obstacles that someone who isn't tech savvy may find overly daunting. We need to make sure that K–12 teachers who want to try these kinds of innovative projects have the technical support they need. The teachers I interviewed for this project, for example, talked about the difficulty of conducting synchronous conversations with global colleagues due to time-zone differences. With most of the world being at least five hours ahead of eastern standard time, one would have to have an early-morning class in the United States to communicate with a class across the world that is still in session. These time-zone challenges make the establishment of a learning platform essential, whether it is a wiki, common blog, or Ning. These venues, while relatively simple to set up, do require at least some knowledge of new media. As I continue to work with teachers across the United States on this topic, they regularly ask the question, "What's a wiki?"—sometimes even young teachers. It is clear from the teachers I interviewed about international collaboration that they came into these projects with a relatively high interest in technology and a willingness to experiment and innovate. While a willingness to experiment and innovate can't necessarily be inculcated in teachers via staff development, it seems that these kinds of global projects, at the very least, will necessitate some professional development for teachers, even just demonstrating the process of setting up a wiki or using Google Earth.

One hopes that teachers and their superiors will invest in this kind of professional development. Teachers seem to be guilt-ridden over what one might call *the entertainment factor* of these new media and worry that by opening up their classrooms to web 2.0 and other new literacies, they disrupt the seriousness of school and dumb it down. All this cyberspace activity is seen as too much fun for kids—with not enough rigor. There may be a continuing perception that these kinds of projects are extras—something to undertake toward the end of the year after students have completed standardized tests. The idea that setting up global collaborations is fluff could not be further from the truth as the United States implements a national curriculum (the Common Core) that emphasizes the need for students to be able to compete and thrive on a global stage.

What's interesting is that in many cases the teachers interviewed for this study were actually working on these global projects outside of the scope of their curriculum maps, perhaps not knowing how much even pre-Common Core standards documents would support their work. (The interviews for this study were completed before the implementation of the Common Core in many areas of the United States.) Many of the teachers interviewed for this study researched, created, and implemented these global awareness projects on their own, apart from any district leadership. The educators were quite passionate about global education and what it can provide for their middle school classrooms. It is clear that they have been committed to what these collaborations can provide to their students—especially as they stay up to very late hours to communicate across many time zones and finish the projects they want to get done.

The teachers I interviewed are struggling with the barriers that we all encounter—lack of technology, lack of support, lack of time, struggles with time zones, and, of course, a continuing societal obsession with standardized curriculum and testing. However, these teachers have persevered. Perhaps a key value of the new media is their ability (via their portability and self-actualization potential) to help break down the walls that separate the classroom from the rest of the world. Brigid Barron's (2006) *learning ecology framework* suggests the value of looking at technology across settings:

> The learning ecology framework draws on ecological perspectives as well as constructs developed from sociocultural and activity theory. Ecological perspectives emerged from a desire to better articulate the interdependencies between child level and environmental variables in development and acknowledge the tight intertwining of person and context in producing developmental change. (p. 196)

The educators interviewed for this study draw on the new media's capabilities for breaking down barriers between classrooms across borders. To return to the work of Friedman (2007), new media creates an unprecedented opportunity to break down the barriers that separate countries and cultures. It would be a shame to not capitalize on the amazing affordances of these new media to reach across the obstacles that separate cultures.

It's hard to believe that the kindergarten students I observed during the 2011–2012 school year will be graduating in June 2024. Those who read this chapter may look back almost nostalgically on a time when people did not have international colleagues and contacts as a part of their daily lives. They may look back and wonder why it took educators so long to take advantage of all the many ways the web provides for reaching across boundaries.

Conclusion

Since September 11, 2001, actual international travel for many people has become more difficult, due to the expense of air travel and the inconvenience of increased security procedures. As I have been writing and thinking about international collaborations, I've thought of my own childhood experiences when international travel seemed much easier and carefree. As a child, I often accompanied my father to the airport with my globetrotting grandmother. I well remember the excitement of being in an airport in the late 1960s and 1970s, as we would escort my grandmother at very early hours, accompanying her to the gate and watching her plane take off. I remember the glamour of travel at that time. My grandmother brought back to us gifts from Spain, Portugal, Japan, and all of the other exotic locales she visited. I still have many of those objects, and they remind me of the lure of foreign lands from my boyhood.

Probably, the comfort level my grandmother and all those who traveled during those years enjoyed will, perhaps, never be replicated for the casual, everyday traveler. The tradeoff is that we live in a world that is easily accessed, if not face-to-face then at least virtually. We need to take advantage of these faraway virtual worlds now at our fingertips.

References and Resources

Barron, B. (2006). Interest and self-sustained learning as catalysts of development: A learning ecology perspective. *Human Development, 49*(4), 193–224.

Delpit, L. (1995). *Other people's children: Cultural conflict in the classroom.* New York: New Press.

Fairclough, N. (1989). *Language and power.* London: Longman.

Fairclough, N. (1995). *Critical discourse analysis: The critical study of language.* New York: Longman.

Freire, P. (1970). *Pedagogy of the oppressed* (M. B. Ramos, Trans.). New York: Continuum.

Friedman, T. L. (2007). *The world is flat: A brief history of the twenty-first century.* New York: Farrar, Straus & Giroux.

Glaser, B. G., & Strauss, A. L. (1967). *The discovery of grounded theory: Strategies for qualitative research.* Chicago: Aldine Press.

International Baccalaureate. (2012). *Mission and strategy.* Accessed at www.ibo.org /mission on August 19, 2013.

Kist, W. (2005). *New literacies in action: Teaching and learning in multiple media.* New York: Teachers College Press.

Kist, W. (2010). *The socially networked classroom: Teaching in the new media age.* Thousand Oaks, CA: Corwin Press.

Kist, W. (2013). *The global school: Connecting classrooms and students around the world.* Bloomington, IN: Solution Tree Press.

Lankshear, C., & Knobel, M. (2003). *New literacies: Changing knowledge and classroom learning.* Buckingham, England: Open University Press.

McLaren, P. (1986). *Schooling as a ritual performance: Towards a political economy of educational symbols and gestures.* London: Routledge.

McLaren, P. (1989). *Life in schools: An introduction to critical pedagogy in the foundations of education.* New York: Longman.

Merriam, S. B. (1998). *Qualitative research and case study applications in education* (2nd ed.). San Francisco: Jossey-Bass.

Morrell, E. (2002). Toward a critical pedagogy of popular culture: Literacy development among urban youth. *Journal of Adolescent and Adult Literacy, 46*(1), 72–77.

Myers, J., & Eberfors, F. (2010). Globalizing English through intercultural critical literacy. *English Education, 42*(2), 148–171.

National Council for the Social Studies. (2010). *National curriculum standards for social studies: A framework for teaching, learning, and assessment.* Silver Spring, MD: Author. Accessed at www.socialstudies.org/standards/strands on August 19, 2013.

National Governors Association Center for Best Practices & Council of Chief State School Officers. (2010). *Common Core State Standards for English language arts and literacy in history/social studies, science, & technical subjects.* Washington, DC: Authors.

New London Group. (1996). A pedagogy of multiliteracies: Designing social futures. *Harvard Educational Review, 66*(1), 60–92.

Partnership for 21st Century Skills. (2011). *Life and career skills.* Accessed at www.p21.org/overview/skills-framework/266 on August 19, 2013.

Prensky, M. (2005). Listen to the natives. *Educational Leadership, 63*(4), 8–13.

Rogers, R. (2002). "That's what you're here for, you're supposed to tell us": Teaching and learning critical literacy. *Journal of Adolescent and Adult Literacy, 45*(8), 772–787.

Short, K. G., & Harste, J. (1996). *Creating classrooms for authors and inquirers* (2nd ed.). Portsmouth, NH: Heinemann.

Willinsky, J. (1990). *The new literacy: Redefining reading and writing in the schools.* New York: Routledge.

Homa Sabet Tavangar, MPA, is the author of *Growing Up Global: Raising Children to Be At Home in the World* (2009), hailed by national education and business leaders and media ranging from Dr. Jane Goodall to the BBC, NBC, ABC, *Washington Post* online, *Chicago Tribune*, *Chicago Sun-Times*, *Boston Globe*, PBS, Scholastic, *Parents*, Rodale, and many more.

Her work is sparking initiatives to help audiences from CEOs to kindergartners learn and thrive in a global context—and have fun along the way. She has been a visiting scholar at the University of Pennsylvania and is a contributor to the *Huffington Post*, PBS, SproutTV, MomsRising, GOOD, Ashoka's Start Empathy initiative, and Edutopia, among other media, and a sought-after speaker and trainer around global citizenship, parenting, globalizing curriculum, empathy, and inclusion. She is coauthor of the forthcoming *The Global Education Toolkit for Elementary Learners* (Corwin, 2014).

Homa has twenty years of experience in global competitiveness and organizational, business, and international development with hundreds of businesses, nonprofit agencies, governments, and international organizations. She has lived on three continents and is a graduate of UCLA and Princeton University's Woodrow Wilson School of Public and International Affairs. She speaks four languages, and her religious heritage includes four of the world's major faiths. She has served on various nonprofit boards, including her current position on the board of directors of the Tahirih Justice Center, a national leader in protecting immigrant women and girls fleeing violence. She is married and the mother of three.

To learn more about Homa's work, visit www.growingupglobal.net.

To book Homa Sabet Tavangar for professional development, contact pd @solution-tree.com.

Chapter 4
Growing Up in a Global Classroom

By Homa Sabet Tavangar

The year is 1910. Imagine a teenage girl living in a village in the Middle East. Here, girls never—ever—learn to read or write. In fact, no one outside of the girl's closest family members had even seen her bare face since she was a young child. Girls from this place meet their husbands on their wedding day, around the age of ten or eleven. This particular girl was feisty and known for her intelligence, so she put her foot down and didn't marry until an almost scandalous age—fifteen. The day she met her husband, she was pleasantly surprised. He seemed kind and was easy on the eyes. She felt like the luckiest girl in the world.

In her universe, her life offered all she expected. She was soon pregnant, and there was peace in her home. Then, one day, during her first pregnancy, her husband announced that he had an important issue to discuss with her parents. The young husband had been out to see more of the world and had decided that his wife should become literate. As the mother of his children, he was convinced their future would look brighter if she could read and write.

What seems like an innocuous proposal now actually scandalized her family. No girls in their clan read on their own—they memorized key sections of the Koran only—and they were not about to rock tradition. His radical ideas could lead to more trouble, so her parents demanded the marriage be dissolved, the child be aborted, and he leave their home and village for good. None of this sat well with their daughter. While she had obeyed her parents on all matters her entire life, for the first time she was ready to disobey them, at any cost. She ran away from her parents' home, found her husband in a nearby town, and—to her great peril—had the child without any family nearby.

The young couple built a new life for themselves. The young mother became functionally literate. What's more, her child—a little girl—grew up to be a prominent educator in Iran. Thanks to the couple's commitment to education and other progressive ideals, their six children who survived to adulthood all thrived. The girl's parents and siblings never welcomed her back to their homes or lives, but she didn't look back.

This girl was my grandmother. In addition to educators, my grandparents' children became engineers, doctors, and active civic contributors. My father came to the United States on a scholarship in the 1960s to pursue a PhD in industrial and organizational psychology. Today, my generation—the grandchildren—live all over the world and are leaders in fields like medicine, telecommunications, public policy, and Internet security. One bold step to unlock the power of education transformed my grandparents' lives and that of the subsequent generations far beyond what anyone could have imagined.

My grandparents' story is extraordinary, in part, because it's really not so uncommon. When I share their experience, listeners often recall their own tales of progress or change. Transformations involving life circumstances, opportunities, and attitudes occur every day, everywhere, and to almost everyone. What once seemed impossible suddenly becomes very real: the child of undocumented workers from Mexico enrolls in a Mandarin language immersion school in Los Angeles, California; four in ten marriages in the United States are comprised of interfaith couples (Pew Forum on Religion & Public Life, 2008); and the basic computing power available on a handheld smartphone—that you use to communicate with friends and family in faraway places—is far greater than NASA's *Apollo 11*.

What Transformative Times Mean for the Classroom

The confluence of so many changes—from lifestyle and ways of thinking to technology use—characterizes the global society we live in and certainly impacts the direction of education. The classroom—the coming together of curricula, the people who make it come alive, and sometimes, though not always, a physical space—serves as a vital starting point for reflecting on, studying, and embracing what it means to be human in the 21st century.

Against the backdrop of constant change and global influence, the global classroom becomes crucial. The dynamic global classroom ideally fosters enthusiasm for learning, creativity, collaboration, new and effective means of communication through diverse channels, inclusive social environments, and meaningful connections with the larger world, as shown in figure 4.1. Growing up in a global classroom, which can look like moving through the formative learning years in a shifting yet nurturing environment, can be one of the greatest, although less-acknowledged, steps toward contributing to a thriving population of students ready to take on the challenges of our present and future.

Figure 4.1: Elements of a global classroom.

Before explaining the individual sections of figure 4.1, I wish to clarify a few key ideas embedded in the model. First, each classroom should *personalize the global*. This means that classrooms should integrate global awareness throughout problem solving, critical thinking, and analysis of information—not keep it in a separate *global* category. This can best begin by starting with interests and strengths students and staff already possess. In other words, start with what you love, such as literature, science, music, art, or sports. Any of these subjects can drive a global exploration that follows a natural progression of inquiry leading to competency.

This starting point acknowledges that many will not feel equipped with enough global expertise. That's OK. Keep remembering your own story of transformation (or gather courage from someone else's), and imagine your job is to nudge along the as-yet-to-be-realized story of your students. The process needs to begin somewhere, however imperfectly. So many impressive global initiatives began under unlikely circumstances. As the elements of the global classroom outlined in this chapter nurtured them, they blossomed into something new, positive, and often unexpected.

Alongside personal or topical interest areas, the schools' vision, mission, and goals should drive the process. Make global learning an explicit, not inferred, goal. This way, the curriculum—not the technology or the shiniest tools—drives an integrative, strategic process. For example, iPads or SMART Boards in the classroom don't drive global connections, but a mission to create global understanding will drive the purchase of the most appropriate tools to fulfill that learning goal.

If learning is to help build a better world, I prefer to work toward thriving or flourishing rather than succeeding. While success often is thought of in materialistic or competitive terms, to thrive encompasses academic and professional benchmarks, as well as social and character development and draws in diverse stakeholders. Martin Seligman (2011), a pioneer in positive psychology, posits that to flourish is the goal in measuring well-being, which includes, but encompasses more than, the attainment of happiness. Flourishing realizes ever-increasing *positive emotion*, *engagement*, *positive relationships*, *meaning*, and *accomplishment* (or PERMA). So, learning in this context, which many students might understand in practice as being a true friend in a wider, global context, is more likely to nurture a dedicated lifelong learner who will make a positive impact on the world.

A Global Citizen: A Friend to the Whole Human Race

At the center of this global classroom model is an alternative to the competitive achievement goal. The concept of friendship closely linked with global citizenship is one I stumbled on while writing *Growing Up Global: Raising Children to Be At Home in the World* (2009), and it became a core principle of the book. As I stated in *Growing Up Global*:

To "be a friend to the whole human race" (Abdu'l-Bahá, 1976, p. 169), a simple yet profound process is launched. One doesn't need to feel the overwhelming burden of trying to teach their children about the whole world. The magic of one close friendship, and the many activities you experience together along the way, will yield its own lessons—naturally. (Tavangar, 2009, p. 3)

In the time since the book's release, I've given many presentations on global citizenship and global education to audiences ranging from K–12 students to corporate CEOs. I ask a version of the same question each time: "How would you describe the qualities of a good friend?" Then, without fail, hands shoot up, and responses flow: *loyal, respectful, caring, considerate, trusting, nonjudgmental, you can tell them anything, they have your back, we have fun*, and so on.

This discussion allows an audience to reflect on a concept as basic and comforting as *friendship*, and it demonstrates something very special: all groups of any age, location, ethnicity, economic background, level of achievement, or belief system define friendship not only with the same ideas but their words stream out virtually in the same order—every single time. Somehow, *loyalty* and *respect* come out first, and almost as an afterthought, someone inserts *fun* as we wind down the discussion. The experience of diverse groups shows two things: (1) we all want to be a friend and to have friends, and (2) definitions and descriptions of friendship are uncannily universal and deceptively simple. The recognition of these characteristics creates a powerful unifying focal point and a building block for what it means to be human across every cultural and social boundary.

When it's time to process the discussion, I relate the qualities of a good friend back to what it means to be a citizen of the world. At the early stages of writing *Growing Up Global*, I struggled to describe what it meant to be a citizen of the world in the United States. For so many Americans, the idea of global citizenship may raise red flags, as a threat to their patriotism. However, the benefits of being global and involved in national and local affairs don't need to be mutually exclusive. In fact, they can support each other. Examining them through a lens of friendship allows people to think more constructively about global identity.

In the context of teaching and learning, being a friend to the whole human race turns an increasingly frantic, us-against-them survival race on its head. Education shifts toward a service goal, rather than a competitive one. At the model's core is the idea of a relationship: interactive, iterative, exciting, forgiving, and lifelong. Likewise, a global citizen enjoys a dynamic relationship with the world, not a static state of being. If students pursue science, reading and writing, mathematics, social studies, music, art, and physical education within a framework of this relationship, they are more likely to be motivated to take on the challenges of our world to solve its problems.

In this model, education occupies a glorified position. A race for high test scores seems like too narrow a goal, limiting what the citizenry might become and their creative ambitions. Educators, parents, policymakers, and students can all begin to envision the types of human beings we need and want to be to create a better world, because we care about it, as a friend cares about her friends' well-being. In turn, this process cultivates meaning, discovery, and joy in our own lives.

Elements of a Global Classroom

Just like talking about the qualities of close friends, building a vocabulary around global citizenship, placing it squarely in the context of learning and being, and checking in on these ideas over the course of each year can build a new mindset that prioritizes alternative learning goals and characteristics that stick for a lifetime. By nature, these elements are dynamic, contributing to and benefitting from each other and to the core of being a friend to the whole human race. They may be understood as follows.

Enthusiasm for Learning

When learning is real, participatory, and relevant, enthusiasm emerges naturally. Project-based learning offers a particularly effective vehicle for instilling this type of learning. This hands-on approach helps students to personalize, visualize, and practice global learning, since they use cross-curriculum and collaboration skills to explore real-world problems and challenges. Through work on multidisciplinary projects, students are more likely to obtain a deeper knowledge of the subjects they're studying, which improves retention of information, and builds confidence and self-direction. These qualities, together with the cognitive, social, and emotional engagement, help build global competency as organizations like the Asia Society and Council of Chief State School Officers define and advocate (Boix Mansilla & Jackson, 2011).

For example, a study of water can focus on its chemical properties and the memorization of concepts like *water cycle*, *water table*, and *sustainability challenges*. Or, take a project-based learning approach: start with learning the properties of water in order to solve or understand a vexing water emergency. Perhaps your school has a partnership or a contact with a school in Pakistan, Kenya, Haiti, or California—or simply spin the globe and pick a spot where your finger lands. You might approach the study of water as an understanding of the contrasting challenges facing your two environments. Getting to the point of asking the right questions is an important early step. Communicate with real people in the location of study about their water challenges. Knowing that the questions will have an actual audience raises the quality of inquiry. These informed questions and responses help formulate a plan of study and action. When action is an end step in the process as opposed to a unit test, and the action can impact people that your students are getting to know through their research or school partnership, students personalize the learning. Studying an issue becomes relevant as a matter of service to a friend. Together, this can ensure and build enthusiasm.

Creativity

A classroom that fosters global understanding and exploration is more likely to nurture creativity in social and academic problem solving, in forms of expression for presentations, in aesthetic sensibilities, and more. To bring out the creative gifts in each student, consider a whole-child, five-senses approach. This is a simple tool I have developed for use in diverse classroom settings. The five senses offer a checklist that is deliberate and thoughtful as well as easy to remember and access. A celebrated and inspirational example we can use is Leonardo da Vinci. Studies examining his life and work style show that he deliberately sharpened and fed all his senses in the service of his scholarly and creative pursuits. As you enrich the creative side of your global classroom, imagine all the future Leonardo da Vincis discovering, fashioning, and generating new ideas by awakening their five senses, as shown in figure 4.2 (pages 74–75).

Collaboration

A global citizen, a friend to the whole human race, has honed his or her ability to collaborate across many boundaries. This can occur between various teachers across the curriculum, among students, and ideally, with classrooms around the world using diverse technologies. Engaging in substantive collaborative projects serves as an important 21st century learning and innovation skill (Partnership for 21st Century Skills, 2011) and is crucial to demonstrating the power of connections toward serving a higher goal.

Without collaboration, a global connection may begin and end with searching for new friends on Facebook or playing multiuser, multilocation videogames with anonymous competitors. With collaboration, classrooms can use gaming or social media productively to participate in global youth advocacy and awareness raising through terrific organizations like One World Youth Project, New Global Citizens, or World Savvy; contribute to the dialogue at a global event like a United Nations Summit with a youth component or a TEDxYouthDay; or "meet" someone living in a place the class is studying through a program like Global

A FIVE-SENSES APPROACH TO A CREATIVE, GLOBAL CLASSROOM

❑ SIGHT—WHAT DO YOU SEE?

A global classroom not only displays a world map prominently but also art and other objects representing diverse cultural aesthetics rotated or showcased throughout the year to demonstrate a range of beauty and visual experiences. Honor cultural resources of families in the class and community, like books written in other alphabets, photography, native dress, home décor, and handicrafts.

I see . . .

❑ HEARING—WHAT DO YOU HEAR?

Ideally, your school teaches world languages, but even without this valuable offering, you can train your ear to recognize new sounds through concerted exposure. This can take so many forms, such as listening to diverse music sung in various languages or in English but with different accents; including foreign language words or phrases during core class activities (for example, learn how to say *history, thank you, travel,* or *conservation,* or learn to count in multiple languages); showing respect for and making an effort to properly pronounce names in the class; and recognizing how members of the school community are treated—are they noticed, ignored, or included?

I hear . . .

❑ TASTE—HOW MANY DIVERSE TASTES HAVE YOU ENJOYED?

Bring new foods to class and encourage treats that reflect the cultures of the class, even if it's just the topping on a cupcake. Celebrate a project culmination with a thematically relevant food, preferably one that is new to most class members.

I taste . . .

❑ TOUCH—CAN YOU TELL WHAT AN OBJECT IS BY ITS TEXTURE?

Da Vinci would sometimes wear velvet while working to kindle his creative process. Display, or preferably use, diverse products like tablecloths, rugs, wall hangings, writing instruments, and food containers (for example, lunchboxes or utensils from around the world), and encourage diverse expressions of cultural clothing, all to stimulate the tactile experience.

I touch . . .

❑ SMELL—DO CERTAIN SCENTS EVOKE A MEMORY?

You can incorporate diverse smells in a classroom with a bit of effort. For example, in a writing station or other quiet area, display one scent at a time—from turmeric to fenugreek to rose water or chili. These scents can prompt an essay or simply be part of a sensory tour in the classroom. Teachers can use smells to discuss how people's perspectives vary widely. For example, the same item, like garlic, can evoke comfort to some while discomfort to others. Include smell as a consideration in writing, science, or social studies.

I smell . . .

Figure 4.2: Five-senses classroom checklist.

Nomads Group, follow causes the class would like to gather more information about, or participate in a whole new social and economic movement revolving around *collaborative consumption* (Botsman, 2010).

Teachers play a crucial role in modeling constructive collaboration. As a goal, each year every teacher can aim for at least one collaborative project, whether it is with another teacher in the building across disciplines, with a resource person in your community, or with an activist or educator across the planet. Engage students in the collaboration, even if it is to discuss the challenge of collaboration.

As these skills become part of the natural flow of learning, important human qualities develop. For example, collaboration calls for flexibility while working with a group, for responsibility to complete your portion, for compassion to understand if the other side doesn't come through as you did, and for resilience to keep moving ahead despite criticisms, technical failures, or cultural misunderstanding. The act of working together on any project helps you recognize assumptions about the other person or group as you grow to understand their different perspectives and priorities. These life skills are among the qualities of a global citizen and a good friend, and 21st century employers seek them.

Effective Communication Through Multiple Channels

Prior to turning my attention to educating and raising global kids, I spent my career working with companies and governments on how they could best compete in global markets. Especially in the early 1990s, when globalization was just starting to take firm hold, most adults were more apprehensive about where to go, what they should say, how they would be received, and what *faux pas* they might make than the kids I knew and continue to meet. However, there was an exception.

Those who had exposure to foreign cultures, whether it was simply the memory of an uncle coming home from his travels and sharing stories with the family or a childhood friend who had emigrated from another country and shared his or her culture openly, had simple advantages over those who didn't grow up imagining and talking about exotic places and cultures. Those who grew up learning a second language or traveling abroad from a young age had the clearest advantages adjusting their products, marketing plans, partnership and employment agreements; negotiating; and complying with government regulations. It's as if their minds were already limber to the stretches that a new market would require.

If Malcolm Gladwell (2008) had studied entrepreneurs venturing to global markets when he wrote *Outliers: The Story of Success*, I'd bet his *10,000 hours rule*—that genius or success comes more from grit, clocking in many (at least ten thousand) hours of practice and exposure to hone a talent or skill, than any natural ability—would hold up among those who have triumphed in international business.

The implications for today's classroom are clear: start now to clock your hours, and get accustomed to global experiences. Economic circumstances largely determined who had such exposure among the leaders I worked with. Elites got to travel, got tutored on a foreign language, and had reading material from diverse perspectives lying around their homes. One reason I made a career transition from international business to global education was to address this gap, so any-one of any means could tap into global experiences. Whether the motivation is economics, social justice, or national security, it's clear that global know-how and communication skills can't remain the exclusive domain of the privileged.

Foreign Language Exposure

Exposure to a foreign language is another beneficial aspect of the global class-room. The American Council on the Teaching of Foreign Languages' (n.d.) meta-analysis highlights the benefits of language learning, including improving students' ability to hypothesize in science; higher scores on the SAT, ACT, and standardized tests; and increased attentional control and other important cogni-tive abilities.

In spite of the overwhelming case for teaching languages from an early age, U.S. schools are going in the opposite direction. According to the Center for Applied Linguistics, "The percentage of elementary and middle schools offering foreign language instruction decreased significantly from 1997 to 2008: from 31 percent to 25 percent of all elementary schools and from 75 percent to 58 percent of all middle schools" (Rhodes & Pufahl, 2009, p. 1). With the recession taking hold after these numbers were collected, it's likely that foreign language offerings have been squeezed further—they have been where I live and in almost every district I've visited since 2009. In spite of the drops at elementary and middle schools, a steady 91 percent of high schools continue to offer foreign languages. Also, remaining steady, based on U.S. Census data from 2000 and 2010, about 9 per-cent of Americans speak a second language (in other words, 91 percent do not).

Given the preponderance of research asserting that for language mastery to stick it needs to be reinforced early and often, the fact that most U.S. students aren't taught foreign languages until their teen years helps explain a vicious cycle of disappointing results (Duke Talent Identification Program, 2011). Additionally, if language programs don't show excellent results, school board members will justifiably ask, "Why invest scarce funds?" Unfortunately, these decision makers rarely speak a second language themselves. Without firsthand experience of suc-cess in this area, they don't know what effective foreign-language learning looks like, so it's easier to drop the line item amidst tough choices, reinforcing a cycle of underfunded, underperforming foreign-language programs. This pattern calls for community members with positive language experience to speak up and get involved in school board planning.

I can't imagine a school district with struggling mathematics results ever elim-inating mathematics instruction in the elementary grades. Similarly, I doubt there's an athlete who expects to play his or her sport competitively or profession-ally who has never exercised before ninth grade. Further, most athletes grow up in active homes. Parents encourage their children and are themselves engaged in some form of sport, and weekends include some degree of athletics from an early age. So, how do we think U.S. children will have a chance at mastering a lan-guage they've never studied before high school or even been exposed to? This is the quandary most U.S. schools find themselves in, and the multilingual silence is becoming deafening (Duke Talent Identification Program, 2011; Rhodes & Pufahl, 2009).

Regardless of the state of the school's foreign language program, teachers can creatively strengthen the diverse means of communication in their global classrooms. Extending the friendship analogy, good friends find many ways to communicate with each other. The following initiatives will raise awareness and curiosity but are not intended to replace a quality world languages curriculum or act as a language exposure program. To get started, try these seven tips for everyday language exposure.

1. **Begin to know what you see:** Post foreign words or phrases throughout the classroom. Exposing students to words in various languages around key concepts the class is studying in core subjects, character development, art, and physical education allows students to begin to know what they see. These words can be based on the various heritages of your students, the composition of the community, places in the news, or any other geo-graphic prompt.

2. **Rally around your friend's language:** Encourage students who study or speak another language to share a phrase or two per day or week. This is not intended to teach the language but to build appreciation for bilingualism and classroom diversity. This might be the first exposure to a second language for many students, and it may embolden the second-language speaker.

3. **Bring those on the outside in:** Invite parents, international students at local colleges, and other community members to present about their lan-guage, preferably tied to a learning unit already taking place, such as in science or mathematics.

4. **Broadcast it:** Some schools have their morning announcements, or a phrase within them, repeated in a second language. This can help English learners feel more welcome and create excitement in other students when they start to recognize familiar words. If the principal or other key leader repeats part of the announcements or a key phrase in a foreign language,

it will stick better and longer. Depending on the school population, announcements can be in Spanish and English or in a monthly or annual rotation of other languages present in the community.

5. **Talk to new friends faraway:** If you are able to set up a partner classroom where students speak a different first language, create opportunities for the students to teach each other new words while they video chat or correspond.

6. **Watch foreign films:** Age-appropriate, subtitled films offer an exciting lens into a new culture. Organizations like Journeys in Film have curricular guides to accompany great foreign films, and I offer a list of age-appropriate films for grades preK and up in chapter 8 of *Growing Up Global* (Tavangar, 2009).

7. **Go beyond the poster and PowerPoint:** Rather than culminate a unit by making another poster, consider making a video; painting a mural; creating a blog, Ning network, or wiki; publishing an ebook; recording a podcast; or communicating with leaders in the field via Twitter, Facebook, Flickr, Instagram, YouTube, email, or Google+ or Skype. Classrooms can compile social media conversations and posts with a narrative tool like Storify. With Storify, a social network service, students can curate a story from around the web, inserting original voices anywhere inside the story or report they create. These diverse means of communication open up possibilities that build on strengths as diverse as the personalities in the room.

Inclusive Social Environments

No classroom can become a global learning space without a deliberate attempt at creating an inclusive environment for learning, doing, and being. Examining the qualities of friendship serves as an important start in this conversation on core classroom values. I've found that too often, adults may assume that K–12 students understand the qualities of a true friend, what positive virtues and values are, and what commendable behavior should look like. Unfortunately, they often don't, and two basic but important pitfalls might be standing in the way.

First, character development efforts, which are increasingly framed as *antiprograms*, are often inherently negative in their approach (for example, they use such language as *antidrugs* or *antibullying*, as opposed to *peacemaking, friendship, inclusion, presence,* and *finding passions*). So, programs often emphasize what we don't want to see, or what not to do, more than make an alternate vision along with strategies of prosocial behavior very clear. We've all been trained this way.

Think of academics and the media, where the traditional study of history progresses from conflict to conflict, and in the media, where negative or sensational news makes the headlines and positive initiatives may get a nod at the close of the nightly news or on the lifestyle pages within a newspaper or blog. The global classroom can turn this approach on its head. We don't aspire to curse the darkness but to shine a light.

Second, the vocabulary of virtues might be assumed, but it isn't explicitly taught. It needs to be. For several years, I have been meeting with a small group of elementary school students around issues of global citizenship and virtues. I've been surprised to find that initially most did not know the meaning of words like *unity* and *virtues*. Once the teacher exposed the meaning, however, the students picked up quickly and when encouraged began to incorporate them into their conversations and observations about the world.

As I have seen repeatedly, classrooms can introduce fixes to these pitfalls simply. Reframe character development around positive language, and regularly incorporate the language of virtues into classwide (and home) discussions and activities. The Virtues Project offers vocabulary and curriculum emphasizing positive universal qualities like encouragement, compassion, flexibility, humility, honor, justice, integrity, and respect (Popov, 1997). Arthur Costa and Bena Kallick's (2009) *Describing 16 Habits of Mind* identifies behaviors that are indicative of the efficient, effective problem solver. These habits, such as persisting, listening to others with understanding and empathy, and responding with wonderment and awe, overlap with the universal virtues, highlighting the fact that profound thinking skills have the power to bring out the best in human qualities.

Point out the habits and qualities when you observe them—in a science discovery, in literature, on the playground. These virtues, like the Golden Rule, form the backbone of core global classroom values, which help build a greater sense of community, and this community can be seen as a microcosm of the world. Talk about that, too. Mindful of these habits and virtues, intelligent communities can be inclusive communities.

Such a positive, virtues-infused, inclusive environment creates the setting that nurtures listening, which in turn helps recognize perspectives, a key ingredient in the framework for global competence (Boix Mansilla & Jackson, 2011). When the classroom is a safe place for the expression of various perspectives—not the domination of a few star students or the recitation of a single correct answer—students can experience the magic of rich discussion and many voices. This in itself can launch a transformative process.

The Thunderbird School of Global Management identifies important virtues in the global mindset model (Najafi Global Mindset Institute, 2010). The model was developed for international business success, yet it's illuminating for a K–12 learning environment that's striving to create an inclusive global classroom. Three broad categories—(1) intellectual capital, (2) psychological capital, and (3) social capital—contain nine key competencies, including *cosmopolitan outlook*, *passion for diversity*, *self-assurance*, *intercultural empathy*, and *interpersonal impact*. Anyone who cares about instilling a global classroom would do well to keep these capabilities in mind not only to ensure the sort of success an MBA program might encourage, but also an effective antibullying, procuriosity, community-building, and cognitive-strengthening strategy.

Meaningful Connections With the Larger World

We often hear the phrase "I friended you on Facebook." Does that mean we are actually friends? Not necessarily. The same is true in classrooms that join Skype or ePals, welcome an exchange student, or fundraise for victims of a natural disaster; although they offer outstanding and increasing levels of engagement with new "friends" from around the world, they do not necessarily create meaningful connections. To create meaningful connections, get started with the following simple guidelines.

- **Start with what you love:** As the one who sets the class tone, the teacher's interest in the global cause, culture, or initiative needs to be sincere; without a genuine interest, connections are unsustainable and unlikely.

- **Engage your senses:** When filling in the five-senses classroom checklist (pages 74–75) with items from around the world, use these as a launching point for finding interests and for exploring their origin.

- **Communicate on a regular basis:** Frequent and brief check-ins with your global partner or project take the pressure off every interaction needing to be an "event" and allow for a more natural discovery process.

- **Put service at the center:** Connections that revolve around service have a greater chance of lasting. You can try to attack world hunger or human trafficking, but you can also look to areas of interest such as soccer, chess, fashion, or hip-hop music. Many organizations work in these areas and provide opportunities for service. An excellent one-stop resource for matching interests with service and providing opportunities is Global-Giving. The site, which is almost like an eBay for philanthropy, contains thousands of projects from around the world that are eager for donors and volunteers. To get started, type a topic of interest—from cooking, baseball, animals, or dance to a more serious issue of concern, like hunger, clean water, or homelessness—or a country name into the search box. Read descriptions of the projects that come up and help your students (in groups or individually) decide if the location (United States as well as overseas) and the description of the problem or solution interest them. In addition to contributing financially in any amount, donors will develop direct contact with the project and the people behind it, and gain as close a connection to the initiative as they wish to have. You can stop there or use the results as a springboard to learn about similar organizations on other websites and gain exposure to a whole field of philanthropy and service that could make a big difference in how students will view the world.

- **Use school fundraising as a win-win-win:** Through organizations like Global Goods Partners, Equal Exchange (http://equalexchange.coop), Greenraising, or Coffee for Water, sales of high-quality items can benefit your school and educate students on an important cause *and* give back to the countries of origin. It's likely your school already is engaged in fundraising; the consciousness of global citizenship can turn an annual necessity into an unforgettable connection with bigger impact. If done in the context of larger learning goals, then the benefit multiplies.

Conclusion

A global classroom—which can be physical or virtual—serves as a home base for exploring our world and our times, for creating community (near or far), and for encouraging individuals to flourish. When being a friend to all is understood synonymously with global citizenship, a relationship to learning and to the world has potential to take hold in hearts, helping to ensure lasting impact.

As with a relationship, challenges will arise, calling for perseverance and patience—not necessarily abandonment. One attempt to integrate global understanding in the classroom may not stick, but a more holistic global classroom model can inspire trying, trying again, changing course, and then trying again. The global classroom model (page 69), with "A Friend to the Whole Human Race" at its core and real skill sets around the perimeter, offers a springboard for creative efforts as unique as every teacher and classroom dynamic. While the model contains multiple prongs, you don't need to attempt all the elements at once to begin building a global classroom. Start with small steps around personal interests. Share your experiences with learning communities like those described elsewhere in this book. Your greatest support might come from individuals whom you have never met, from somewhere you have never been, and from mentors and cheerleaders from the wider networks you tap into.

When woven into the tapestry of the class, global awareness and sensitivity start to emerge like an instinct applied to almost any issue. Amidst economic crises, social insecurity, and political upheavals, raising a generation with the capacities of global citizenship becomes crucial—not out of fear for the future or a one-dimensional demand to compete but for a love for humanity, a better world, and optimism that together we can solve problems. Remembering the overwhelming obstacles those before us surmounted, we can remain hopeful that the possibility of transformation lies within each one of us. The transformation's setting can be diverse—from a village like my grandmother's to your own classroom—but will open up untold possibilities for learning and friendship with the whole human race.

References and Resources

'Abdu'l-Bahá. (1978). *Selections from the writings of 'Abdu'l-Bahá.* Haifa, Israel: Bahá'í World Centre.

American Council on the Teaching of Foreign Languages. (n.d.). *What does research show about the benefits of language learning?* Accessed at www.actfl.org/i4a/pages /index.cfm?pageid=4524 on March 19, 2013.

Boix Mansilla, V. B., & Jackson, A. (2011). *Educating for global competence: Preparing our youth to engage the world.* New York: Asia Society. Accessed at http://asia society.org/files/book-globalcompetence.pdf on June 19, 2012.

Botsman, R. (2010). *Collaborative consumption hub.* Accessed at www.collaborative consumption.com/the-movement on March 19, 2013.

Costa, A. L., & Kallick, B. (2009). *Describing 16 habits of mind.* Accessed at www.instituteforhabitsofmind.com/resources/pdf/16HOM.pdf on March 19, 2013.

Duke Talent Identification Program. (2011). *Cognitive benefits of learning languages.* Accessed at www.tip.duke.edu/node/866 on August 7, 2013.

Gladwell, M. (2008). *Outliers: The story of success.* New York: Little, Brown.

Najafi Global Mindset Institute. (2010). *Global mindset inventory.* Accessed at http://globalmindset.thunderbird.edu/home/global-mindset-inventory on June 30, 2012.

Partnership for 21st Century Skills. (2011). *Framework for 21st century learning.* Accessed at www.p21.org/storage/documents/1.__p21_framework_2-pager.pdf on March 19, 2013.

Pew Forum on Religion and Public Life. (2008). *U.S. religious landscape survey: Chapter 2—Changes in Americans' religious affiliation.* Accessed at http://religions.pewforum .org/pdf/report-religious-landscape-study-chapter-2.pdf on June 19, 2012.

Popov, L. K. (1997). *The family virtues guide: Simple ways to bring out the best in our children and ourselves.* New York: Plume.

Rhodes, N. C., & Pufahl, I. (2009). *Foreign language teaching in U.S. schools: Results of a national survey.* Washington, DC: Center for Applied Linguistics. Accessed at www.cal.org/resources/pubs/fl_teaching.html on March 19, 2013.

Seligman, M. E. P. (2011). *Flourish: A visionary new understanding of happiness and well-being.* New York: Free Press.

Tavangar, H. S. (2009). *Growing up global: Raising children to be at home in the world.* New York: Ballantine Books.

Heidi Hayes Jacobs, EdD, is an internationally recognized expert in the fields of curriculum and instruction. She writes and consults on issues and practices pertaining to curriculum mapping, dynamic instruction, and 21st century strategic planning. She is president of Curriculum Designers and director of the Curriculum 21 Project, whose faculty provides professional development services and support to schools and education organizations. Featured prominently as a speaker at conferences, at workshops, and on webinars, Heidi is noted for her engaging, provocative, and forward-thinking presentations. She has published eleven books, as well as journal articles, online media, and software platforms. Above all, Heidi views her profession as grounded in a K–12 perspective thanks to her early years as a high school, middle school, and elementary teacher in Utah, Massachusetts, Connecticut, and New York.

Heidi completed her doctoral work at Columbia University's Teachers College, where she studied under a national Graduate Leadership Fellowship from the U.S. Department of Education. Her master's degree is from the University of Massachusetts Amherst, and she did her undergraduate studies at the University of Utah. She is married, has two adult children, and lives in Rye, New York.

To learn more about Heidi's work, visit www.curriculum21.com and follow her on Twitter @curriculum21 and @heidihayesjacob.

To book Heidi Hayes Jacobs for professional development, contact pd @solution-tree.com.

Chapter 5
Interdisciplinary Global Issues: A Curriculum for the 21st Century Learner

By Heidi Hayes Jacobs

Imagine a geography class with a group of eager students in ancient Babylon. The year is 600 BCE, where the Imago Mundi, one of the first maps of the world carved on a thick stone tablet, is the focus of the lesson. Babylon is in the center of the map, located on the Euphrates River, and the adjacent land area shows Assyria and Armenia. Encapsulating the land is Oceanus, translated as the *bitter river*, a reference to some sampled saltiness. There are seven islands in Oceanus that form a seven-pointed star (Unger, 1996). The image of the known world fascinates the young students in the class.

Flash forward to a high school freshman, Tanya, who is holding a different kind of tablet, gliding her finger over Google Earth to locate the Euphrates River. Simultaneously, she obtains topographical and demographic information immediately through a hyperlink. As Tanya opens up the hyperlinks and studies the resultant maps, she is stunned to learn that this is where the Iraq War was fought. Her teacher directs her to a scientific journal, *Water Resources Research*, from which Tanya learns that Iraq's water sources are currently drying up.

Although centuries separate them, Tanya and her ancient Babylonian counterparts have a fundamental commonality: what they know about or have experienced of the world impacts their educational experiences. This leads us to ask ourselves as educators what we must do to upgrade our curriculum practices to cultivate contemporary global citizens. How can we equip our youth to participate in a world that has changed dramatically and that will continue to change at a rapid pace?

We are fortunate to live in a time when virtual contact has opened up new portals for our students. Personalizing a global curriculum is now possible through point-to-point contact using online conferencing tools in real time, making connections between classrooms around the world possible. It is a time of great possibilities and challenges. In order to provide practical guidance on how to inject global literacy into learning experiences and sustain it, my focus will be on three curriculum design considerations.

1. Global literacy relies on content knowledge and the ability to decode maps and embrace geographic vernacular to lay a foundation for linking people to place. We need to refresh the older approaches and standards to teaching geography.

2. Curriculum designers can support global literacy through deliberate integration within disciplines. When the prefix *geo-* is deliberately added to any subject-area topic, there is rich potential for expanding perspectives and adding complexity to units and courses.

3. Curriculum designers can support global literacy through interdisciplinary curriculum design by engaging in thoughtful investigation of selected contemporary global issues, thus preparing our learners for their future.

To elaborate on these three points, we will begin by defining global literacy for curriculum design application. Then, we will examine the first consideration: we will discuss the role of basic geographical terminology for map decoding and how it needs to be linked to the subject areas. Next, we will explore the second consideration regarding approaches to integrating global literacy. Last, sample interdisciplinary units of study will demonstrate what global literacy might look like in classroom practice. To assist educators in making these critical instructional choices, I have developed criteria for selecting the *organizing centers* for interdisciplinary global issues. Let us begin by crafting an operational definition of global literacy for curriculum design purposes.

Defining Global Literacy

Unlike the other literacies, digital and media, *global literacy* relies less on tools and means. We would not call an aspiring reader *literate* if he or she can simply decode sounds or identify the alphabet; a literate person must know how to read. Similarly, just finding a place on a map does not equal global literacy. Global literacy incorporates aspects of digital and media literacy. For example, *digital literacy* includes the ability not only to access but also to strategically select and use a wide array of applications and interactions. *Media literacy* involves responding to and creating media in any and all subjects. The globally literate individual possesses current knowledge about the world, has the ability to connect people to places, and can develop informed opinions regarding contemporary issues.

An intriguing point here is that the use of both digital and media literacy tools can provide a portal to learning more about place and people and therefore contribute to knowledge about the human condition. In other words, having the ability to use Google Earth, search immediate information about a specific location and its people digitally, and view media sources regarding a place supports the development of global literacy. Global studies are inherently interdisciplinary. Globally literate people must go beyond decoding language to accessing information; they must be able to make connections and meaning. Interdisciplinary global studies of contemporary issues are an integral component of global literacy. In order to thoughtfully consider perspectives and procedures for crafting interdisciplinary work, let us begin by considering the baseline discipline focused on the study of the Earth: geography. The goal is not simply to review the fundamentals—but to refresh them.

Refreshing the Fundamentals of Geography

For many students, geography equals boredom. This phenomenon is often the result of a dated model for teaching geography: students decode maps by memorizing geographical terms (*isthmus* and *peninsula*, for example), identifying the seven continents by name, and locating individual countries. This level of geographical decoding is akin to learning the alphabet as a stepping stone to reading a book. To develop global literacy, students must go further—to consistently link people to the places on the map. In his article "Faces, Places, Spaces: The Renaissance of Geographic History," Adam Gopnik (2012) writes, "The history of places, where the ingathering of people and classes in a single city or state makes a historical whole bigger than any one face within it" (p. 108). He goes on to emphasize the indelible notion that "the history of spaces [is] the history of terrains and territories, a history where plains and rivers and harbors shape the social place that sits above them or around them" (p. 108).

Our students need to comprehend the link between faces, places, and spaces as Gopnik describes. We have an opportunity to upgrade geography to global literacy by stepping out of the *pro forma* geography unit of old. In truth, the pedagogy of the past did not intend to isolate geography instruction, as the National Geography Standards indicate (Geography Education Standards Project, 1994).

Revisiting the National Geography Standards

When the Geographic Education Standards Project released the National Geography Standards in 1994, there were no Google Maps or handheld devices. The fundamental purpose of these standards was to cultivate understanding about the relationship between places and people. In 2012, the second edition of the standards, *Geography for Life: National Geography Standards*, was released (Heffron & Downs, 2012). The similarities and differences between the two editions are revelatory. Both sets of standards establish grades 4, 8, and 12 learning targets in a traditional format. Both editions have frameworks comprised of two levels that include six essential elements and eighteen standards. Each essential element is a central outcome of the standards, which consist of related ideas and approaches to geography education. The six essential elements are as follows:

1. The world in spatial terms
2. Places and regions
3. Physical systems
4. Human systems
5. Environment and society
6. The uses of geography

Figure 5.1 (pages 91–92) lists the eighteen standards (Heffron & Downs, 2012).

Examining the National Geography Standards can provide potential 21st century learning targets. Note the range of language patterns.

- Two standards start with the words "How to apply . . ."
- One standard starts with the words "How to analyze . . ."
- Two standards start with the words "How to use . . ."
- One standard starts with "To apply geography to interpret . . ."

None of the standards are complete sentences; rather, they are the seeds of concepts that might follow a predicate such as, "Students will examine . . ." or "Students will describe . . ." For example, standard fifteen might be completed in this way: "Students will investigate how physical systems affect human systems." In short, there is a great deal of latitude as to how teachers can develop these standards, which can inspire creative and engaging curriculum. With this in mind, one of the most significant differences from the past to the present standards is the explicit description of performance statements and sample tasks. Ultimately, the goal of the standards is to cultivate "the geographically informed person" (Heffron & Downs, 2012, p. 7).

We desire that our students not only know geographic terms but employ them as they consider the implications of what they see on a map. The key is to make geography language come alive. In discussing the role of borders, for example, Gopnik (2012) notes:

> And yet these arbitrary lines make cultures as much as they express them. The Canadian-American border, the longest border in the world between two countries, is as willful an act of imagination as a work of conceptual curtaining by Christo, but its existence has made two separate peoples with two separate stories. (p. 114)

We need our learners to not only locate a place but also analyze the relationship between the climate, topography, and resources and the economy and social organization of the people who live there. We need our learners to develop global competence.

THE GEOGRAPHICALLY INFORMED PERSON KNOWS AND UNDERSTANDS . . .

The World in Spatial Terms

1. How to use maps and other geographic representations and technologies to acquire, process, and report information from a spatial perspective

2. How to use mental maps to organize information about people, places, and environments in a spatial perspective

3. How to analyze the spatial organization of people, places, and environments on Earth's surface

Places and Regions

4. The physical and human characteristics of places

5. That people create regions to interpret Earth's complexity

6. How culture and experience influence people's perception of places and regions

Continued →

Figure 5.1: The National Geography Standards

Source: Heffron, S. G., & Downs, R. M. (Eds.). (2012). Geography for life: National Geography Standards, *(2nd ed.).* Washington, DC: National Council for Geographic Education. Reprinted with permission.

Physical Systems

7. The physical processes that shape the patterns of the Earth's surface
8. The characteristics and spatial distribution of ecosystems and biomes on the Earth's surface

Human Systems

9. The characteristics, distribution, and migration of human populations on Earth's surface
10. The characteristics, distribution, and complexity of Earth's cultural mosaics
11. The patterns and networks of economic interdependence on Earth's surface
12. The process, patterns, and functions of human settlement
13. How forces of cooperation and conflict among people influence the division and control of Earth's surface

Environment and Society

14. How human actions modify the physical environment
15. How physical systems affect human systems
16. The changes that occur in the meaning, use, distribution, and importance of resources

The Uses of Geography

17. How to apply geography to interpret the past
18. To apply geography to interpret the present and plan for the future

Developing Global Competencies

The Council of Chief State School Officers and the Asia Society partnered on a project—EdSteps—to develop a set of global competencies, which they released in 2010. The Global Competence Matrix was created as part of the Council of Chief State School Officers' EdSteps Project in partnership with the Asia Society Partnership for Global Learning (Council of Chief State School Officers, 2010). I had the good fortune of participating in their workgroup to create a framework describing and detailing the four competencies: (1) investigate the world, (2) recognize perspectives, (3) communicate ideas, and (4) take action. (Anthony W. Jackson and Veronica Boix Mansilla examine these four competencies in detail in chapter 1 of this book. See page 5.) In my view, these competencies build on the work reflected in the National Geography Standards. The global competency framework provides a solid foundation for cultivating necessary proficiencies. Curriculum planners might question how to integrate the competencies in their content, units, courses, and learning experiences. A natural question a teacher might ask is, "Should my students work within a discipline or across subjects?" For example, a second-grade teacher might decide to concentrate her unit of study of folktales in literature with a social studies unit on the cultures and people who created the stories, and a physics teacher might integrate experiments on trajectory with applications in sports. The possibilities for linkages are rich and abundant in the curriculum. The question is, when and how do we create meaningful connections? We might look to the ancient Greeks for some direction.

The father of geography is considered to be the Greek Eratosthenes (276 BCE–195 BCE). Not only was he the first to use the word *geography*, but he actually cultivated the discipline as a field of study. It is acknowledged that he developed a map of the known world using parallels and meridians and calculated a remarkably accurate circumference of Earth. What struck me as of particular interest is that, according to the Suda, a 10th century Byzantine encyclopedia, Eratosthenes was commonly known by the name *Beta* from the second letter of the Greek alphabet (Asimov, 1982). The nickname emerged because he was considered the second best in the ancient Greek world in almost every field. Eratosthenes was a mathematician, poet, astronomer, science chronologist, athlete, and music theorist. Because of his fascination with the world, he strikes me as an exemplary interdisciplinarian.

Just as Eratosthenes engaged in a wide range of subject areas, we can, in this same spirit, connect many fields of study; there is a natural alliance between geography and other contemporary areas of study. As a curriculum designer, there are two fundamental angles to consider when calibrating the impact of merging geography—the study of Earth—with other content.

1. Look at a specific discipline through a global lens and consider how that view expands topics within a field. In other words, infuse the prefix *geo-* into the disciplines.

2. Rather than commencing with a subject, begin instead with the selection of specific interdisciplinary global issues as organizing centers for design. In other words, upgrade to interdisciplinary unit designs.

Both are legitimate options for curriculum designers and merit reflection as a way to expand and refine the study of geography to infuse global competency. As Boix Mansilla and Jackson (2011) state:

> Rigorous disciplinary understanding requires that students come to view the disciplines as the knowledge and thinking tools that our societies construct and revise to make sense of the world, explain phenomena, solve problems, create products, and ask novel questions in informed ways. (p. 27)

Infusing *Geo-* Into the Disciplines

For curricular purposes, teachers can cultivate globally literate learners by infusing geography into the disciplines—by adding the prefix *geo-*, so to speak. Here are some brief examples of how adding a global perspective begins to expand a typical topic.

- ***Geo*graphy:** Studying borders, topography, and the writing and reading of maps is the basis of geography. Adding the study of demographics and the environment provides a global perspective to traditional geography studies. A dynamic website that provides striking visual displays of data is National Geographic's EarthPulse (www.nationalgeographic.com/earth pulse/index.html).

- ***Geo*-economics:** Technological advances since the mid-1990s have inextricably linked economies around the globe. Globally competent learners must move beyond simplistic supply-and-demand lessons to study global production and the interaction between governments, as well as the inter-relationships between people, resources, places, and currencies. One of the most popular and accessible interactive sites is Hans Rosling's Gapminder (www.gapminder.org). In particular, students can create comparative graphs based on specific indicators such as gender equality in education or health support systems in the data tab (www.gapminder .org/data).

- ***Geo*communications:** The notion of communications has been a fixture of curriculum study as students have learned to write correspondence and use speech as a persuasive tool. Now we have the opportunity for expansive global reach from any classroom. Internet, smartphones, Facebook, Skype, Twitter, and other forms of social media have created instant interpersonal communications that result in rapid news cycles and virtual political movements.

- *Geo*-**arts and literature:** People around the world have long shared their unique perspectives, feelings, and ideas through a variety of artistic media—from visual to performing arts. It can be said that art connected people from different places and backgrounds long before we had shared playlists; however, traditional approaches (such as performances and gallery exhibitions) were limited by space. Now we have new tools and platforms that support immediate access and allow emerging artists to share with an almost unimaginably large virtual audience.

- *Geo*health: Heath has been a basic feature of the curriculum, whether taught by a specialist, a health-care professional, a science teacher, a counselor, or in physical education. Since the 1990s, an emphasis on wellness and lifelong health habits has been prominent in our school programs. Because of our digital and media access, we can share global perspectives on important health issues, such as with the World Health Organization podcasts and RSS feed (http://who.int). The study of health benefits from global connectivity on multiple levels. Whether it is a medical student in Canada observing a real-time surgical procedure in Bangkok or the availability of global community support groups for specific health issues, infusing global elements into health curricula has changed the educational landscape.

- *Geo*sports: It used to be that global sporting events like the Olympics were the only ways students were exposed to international sports. With the development of video technology and access to sports and sporting events all over the world on the Internet, students can learn about sports popular in other places. They can connect with other learners in faraway places who follow specific sports and learn about the role of gender, history, climate, and traditions on how people throughout the world engage in athletics.

- *Geo*-**education:** Ironically, when it comes to our own professional field of practice, educators do very little about studying education with our learners. There may be brief discussions and descriptions of schools in other countries, but we do not investigate the actual pedagogy and range of learning approaches on a global level. Whether literally reading about other countries (as in Vivien Stewart's [2012] *A World-Class Education*) or viewing media (as in the film *Two Million Minutes: A Global Examination* [2008]), a global perspective can promote analysis of what learning looks like in other places. Examining the way children learn in different countries can be fascinating. For example, students in the United States might be surprised to learn that there are no tests given in Finland, or that Singapore has a 220-day school year.

The injection of classical geography into subject areas coupled with digital and media tools can generate compelling investigation within a subject. But this does raise practical questions. There are seemingly endless choices for fields of study but limited hours in the school day. When faced with such abundance, how do you make wise choices regarding curriculum?

Over the years, I have come to rely on three fundamental interrogatives—three basic, down-to-earth considerations that curriculum designers will ask: (1) What do we cut? (2) What do we keep? (3) What do we create? In curriculum design, we are always wrestling with not only what we will include, but what we will have to leave out. When making curricular selections and revisions to courses and units of study, it is imperative we retain a global perspective. Our curriculum should also employ new tools and techniques to match the needs of our learners. Twenty-first century classrooms should not be engaged in geography studies of a bygone era.

Upgrading to Interdisciplinary Unit Design

To support the process of updating curriculum for the 21st century, I advocate a process of upgrading curriculum units as described in *Curriculum 21: Essential Education for a Changing World* (Jacobs, 2010). Upgrading entails the replacement of dated content and assessment within an existing curriculum with modern and current content and assessments. Teachers identify specific units or courses in their curriculum maps and revise them with timely alternatives. In order to develop globally literate learners, educators can make curriculum compellingly relevant by shifting the focus of content to contemporary global issues and problems, as highlighted in the previous section.

It has long been my contention that there is an intrinsic need to create "organizing centers" that naturally cut across discipline lines to foster natural connectivity between subject-area perspectives. Focused, purposeful interdisciplinary design is a formidable approach when there are natural connections between disciplines, such as considering an essential problem, issue, or theme (Jacobs, 1989).

Global issues are inherently interdisciplinary, and they present an opportunity to engage students in problems and topics that will, by necessity, draw on both digital tools and media material. An interdisciplinary global curriculum is vital for students who are immersed in the flow of world events and trends. As Sunaina Maira (2004) writes:

> Youth culture is often taken to be the exemplary manifestation
> of globalization, a testament to its possibilities and excesses,

highlighting the deep anxieties and desires it evokes. Nike-clad or henna-painted, underground, or hypervisible, apathetic, or idealist, anarchist, or apolitical, youth culture seems to be a primary site onto which the dualities used to structure the popular discourse of globalization are projected. (p. 203)

Our units of study need an upgrade to match learners who are going home to play video games with students on the other side of the world who are visiting Facebook pages committed to their favorite political movements.

A Contemporary Interdisciplinary Option

When upgrading content, educators need to thoughtfully re-evaluate subject matter to determine if it is timely and essential. To assist in making curriculum decisions, I developed a continuum of interdisciplinary options—from discipline-based curriculum design to complete-program curriculum design—that identifies the possibilities when creating an interdisciplinary curriculum (see figure 5.2, page 98). The model helps a curriculum designer choose the degree of integration that is appropriate for a given learning situation. This model can be applied to the development of global interdisciplinary units and is a dynamic way to support globally literate learners.

In a *discipline-based curriculum*, students do not simply study geography—they act as geographers and use the contemporary tools of geographers. In the *parallel-discipline approach*, teachers in different disciplines attend to global studies in a concurrent time frame, but still within their individual subjects. There are no formal connections between the subjects in this approach, thus leaving students to make the connections. *Multidisciplinary design* is when one or two subjects are linked formally in an investigation, which provides opportunities to deepen global learning, such as when history and geography are combined in the examination of a region. *Interdisciplinary unit design* employs a wide range of disciplines in the thoughtful examination of one organizing center (or hub for investigation) while simultaneously engaging in an expanded examination. To be clear, interdisciplinary unit design formally cuts across subjects and is different from a parallel unit design, which does not purport to link disciplines formally. *Integrated day models* are in nontraditional scheduled schools, where there are no divisions between disciplines, and the focus is on immediate and present themes or problems. *Complete program curriculum planning* occurs when a setting is fully integrated—such as with a group of learners going on an Outward Bound experience. Thus, interdisciplinary design is the most practical and actionable choice to cultivate global literacy within units or courses. With this type of design, you must first select global organizing centers.

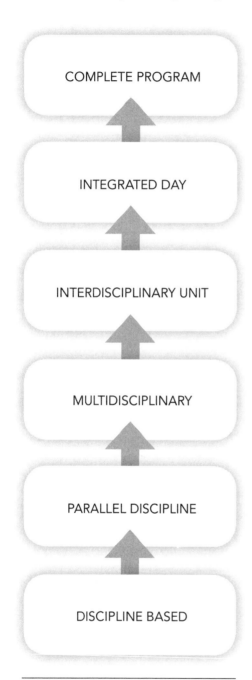

Figure 5.2: Continuum of options for content design.

Source: Jacobs, 1989.

Criteria for Selecting Global Interdisciplinary Organizing Centers and Digital Tools

How do we choose worthy organizing centers for the upgraded curriculum? The organizing center is the hub for investigation. In their discussion of quality interdisciplinary understanding, Veronica Boix Mansilla and Anthony W. Jackson (2011) suggest that effective units are purposeful, grounded in disciplines, integrative, and thoughtful. They raise a fundamental point and encourage us to stop and reflect before we roll up our sleeves and act. In particular, I would suggest that their first and third features have bearing on making our work timely. We need *purposeful* and forward-looking units that *integrate* modern media and digital tools. It should be requisite for curriculum designers to directly embed interactive digital tools and resources into upgraded units of study.

As I have worked with teachers in various settings from preK through higher education, I have seen that selecting an organizing center is fraught with potential problems for professional developers. With good intentions, a planning team might grab onto a current or passing trend to create a token global-studies experience. The following are a set of curriculum-crafting criteria, contemporary planning tenets, if you will, for globalizing learning. The goal is to shape a meaningful learning experience through a thoughtfully planned unit of study. Ask yourself these questions as you consider which global aspects to include in your curriculum.

1. Does this unit prompt investigation of a relevant issue, topic, or problem? Does it require an international perspective? Not every issue in the news or in a textbook has global ramifications, but many of them do. Organizing centers need to have clear global linkages.

2. Will this unit promote an understanding of immediate local issues, topics, or problems that naturally connect to the larger global situation? Does this curricular plan allow students to personalize the global?

3. Does the organizing center for the unit of study elicit a connection between individual students in one country with individual students in another? Whether establishing a virtual connection via Skype, promoting an ePal relationship, or actually visiting another country, there is nothing that compares to human contact.

4. Does this unit instigate research on a long-term environmental impact that transcends national lines and reflects political realities?

5. Does the organizing center for the unit connect the cause-and-effect relationship of place and human activity? Social, economic, political, or health issues exemplify these relationships.

6. Does the organizing center for the unit support fruitful study of the current topics relevant for each discipline?

7. Does this curricular element stimulate a look at career and college readiness by either taking action on a global issue or a locally connected issue while linking the student with adult professionals working on solutions?

8. Does the unit integrate digital tools seamlessly and purposefully to support investigation?

9. Does it generate opportunities for responding to global media sources and creating media projects?

10. Does this curricular unit provide lifelong capacity for mindful, personal development and community well-being?

Your group may choose to revise these criteria or adopt a different set; regardless, it is important to have a selection process in place. Otherwise, individuals will tend to gravitate to areas of personal interest rather than what students actually need to learn. The goal is to ensure that contemporary themes and issues replace some of the more dated content our learners are presently studying.

Examples of Engaging Global Interdisciplinary Organizing Centers

Let us consider some examples of contemporary global interdisciplinary organizing centers that I have gathered over the years (Jacobs, 2010). The following unit concepts include a big idea (a targeted issue, problem, case study, or theme), an essential question to frame inquiry, and a description of how these are translated into practice as a unit of study. These are some examples of what planning teams might come up with to upgrade the curriculum to nurture globally literate learners.

Environmental Awareness: Sustaining the World in My Own Backyard

Big idea: Sustainability involves learning to make decisions that provide for the needs of the world's current population without damaging the ability of future generations to provide for themselves. Sustainability encompasses the intertwined ideals of viable economies, equity and justice, and ecological integrity (Washington Center, 2008).

Essential questions: How does human activity impact the stability and diversity of ecosystems? How are people making choices to sustain the world locally and globally?

Translation into practice: Examining how to preserve and support our planet's resources is central to our survival as a species. Whether it is a second-grade class in Newark, New Jersey, learning how to become Planet Protectors or a high school class in Chicago designing alternative energy sources for third-world countries, sustainability is a critical subject for interdisciplinary investigation. It entails extensive statistical analysis, study of life and earth sciences, and study of community values and laws. The unit might involve the following organizations.

Facing the Future (www.facingthefuture.org), a Seattle-based nonprofit, provides outstanding curriculum materials on climate change, population growth, poverty, environmental degradation, and global health crises. Facing the Future's textbook resource, *Exploring Global Issues: Social, Economic, and Environmental Interconnections* (2013), provides an active approach to society's "collective impact."

Inhabitat (http://inhabitat.com) provides a forum for investigating emerging trends in eco-architecture, sustainable design innovation, and green building. The Cloud Institute for Sustainability Education (www.sustainabilityed.org) focuses on developing student leadership programs in schools to promote sustainability. The realities of cultural adaptation, the deployment of statistical data, the investigation of physical geography, and the implications both politically and economically regarding environmental policy are an integral part of the Cloud Institute's curriculum approach.

Global Ambassador: A Connector of Cultures

Big idea: In an interactive global environment, economic and political survival relies on cultural understanding, language facility, and geographic knowledge to support international cooperation.

Essential questions: What connects people from different places, and what separates them? How can I become a global ambassador?

Translation into practice: Becoming globally literate requires a new commitment to applied geography and an understanding of the role it plays in economic and social development. Encouraging our learners to become ambassadors creates an opportunity to extend their worldview and personalize global issues. This personalization means that students acquire concrete knowledge and direct experience with students from other parts of the world via video conferencing and regular web-based interactions (Committee for Economic Development, 2006). Teachers from Australia and the United States started the Global Classroom Project to connect classrooms in a personal and academic forum. The key to becoming an ambassador is to engage in dialogue and joint projects. This program provides a natural venue. Another organization that creates relationships is the Peace Corps Coverdell World Wise Schools program (wws.peacecorps .gov/wws/index.cfm?), which has free resources for U.S. classroom teachers to draw from that address the challenge of bringing people from different countries together who are struggling with basic local survival issues, such as access to water, cultivating crops, microfinancing, and literacy. One of the most personalized curriculum projects supporting the idea of studying and understanding a range of individuals worldwide is the 100 People: A World Portrait sponsored by the Gates Foundation (www.100people.org). The concept focuses on the question, "What if the world was a global village represented by one hundred people? What might we learn?" The idea was inspired by an article written in 1990 by Dartmouth professor Donella Meadows (Meadows, 1990). Another leader in proactively assisting schools in connecting cultures is the Asia Society Partnership for Global Learning, which provides a wide range of support. Their Asia Society Education Resources for Schools provide vast curriculum materials and free books and lesson plans (http://asiasociety.org/education/resources-schools/term).

Massive Media: Everybody's News

Big idea: Mass media informs and frames our understanding of the news both locally and globally. Media "mediates" real experience and conveys specific images, sounds, and text to recipients. It is critical to be media literate in order to sift through media sources. Social media now makes it possible for individuals to share their perception of a news event to the larger world instantly, creating a massive media experience.

Essential question: How does mass media shape my perspectives of the world?

Translation into practice: Social media, television, and programs infiltrate our students' lives. We need to create curriculum opportunities on two levels: one level cultivates critically responsive learners who challenge the validity of sources even as they absorb a wide range of viewpoints, and the other level promulgates professional, career-oriented pathways to generate global media, such as becoming a professional news reporter. Global journalism is about the business of fostering new perspectives on local events as seen through a worldwide lens. The global reporting work of the Pulitzer Center (http://pulitzercenter.org) provides students with a running account of current news stories ranging from "Former Rio Slums Attract Hip Europeans Looking for Cheap Housing" (Llana, 2012) to "Russia's Booming Nuclear Industry" (Conant, 2012). The education tab on their website provides thoughtfully developed units of study for classroom application to examine the choices journalists make in sharing stories with a worldwide audience. The California-based Center for Media Literacy (www.medialit.org) has developed effective programs to directly assist K–12 teachers with engaging students in a critical response to the images and messages that bombard them.

Whether it is learning to discern the way a television camera frames an image to affect our view of the news or finding ways to create a film version of a short story, our learners need to study media in order to not become passive recipients. Frank W. Baker's Media Literacy Clearinghouse for educators (www.frankwbaker.com) is an inventive, powerful, and popular source for teachers. Baker breaks down the ways print and visual media journalism shape our worldviews, from the way the cameraman holds the camera to air-brushing the images of politicians. The National Association for Media Literacy Education (www.namle.net) has a wealth of interdisciplinary resources as well as research to guide programs of study. It is astonishing that so few early childhood programs guide our youngest learners in coping with the extraordinary grip that television plays in their lives. It is critical that we upgrade our curricula to equip students with better media skills for viewing, absorbing, and responding to media.

Cities Reimagined: Urban Planning Now and Into the Future

Big idea: New solutions for urban planning are necessary to provide people with a better quality of life.

Essential question: How can we make our cities more livable?

Translation into practice: According to the United Nations Department of Economic and Social Affairs, the global population is over 6.6 billion with more than half of the population living in cities (United Nations, 2011). Urban life brings new pressures on basic services, such as transportation, health care, security, and sanitation. Population growth requires long-term planning to rethink the use of urban spaces for housing, commuting, and access to food. Interdisciplinary in nature, urban studies prompt students to consider new types of urban planning, fresh aesthetic perspectives, new architecture, engineering solutions, and economic and political approaches by government and private sector services. These studies involve the application of scientific research from physics and geology coupled with applied mathematics and with an eye for artful design. Particularly well-suited to exciting integrated curriculum projects are urban planning organizations such as the GOOD Project: Design a Livable Street. Another way of exposing our students to this issue is viewing short video clips documented worldwide through the Street Films project (www.streetfilms.org) and funded by the nonprofit organization OpenPlans (http://openplans.org). Viewing the student-produced films provides students with an insight as to how mass transportation and urban bicycle pathways are becoming part of long-term urban planning. Our young learners are involved in programs such as the Streets Education project based in New York City, which has created interdisciplinary guides and units for early childhood curriculum (*Getting Around, Using Your Street Smarts,* and *Bridges and Tunnels* [http://streetseducation.org/zozo/for-educators]).

Secondary students are dealing with issues of community stewardship. A range of organizations work to develop responsibility and citizenship in caring for local communities. Urban areas prize city parks, and stewardship of these parks is supported by the National Fish and Wildlife Foundation (www.nfwf.org/Pages/com munitystewardship/home.aspx). A global perspective from Europe is available from Urban Projects Europe (http://urbact.eu), which provides a detailed list and links to specific urban renewal projects throughout Europe with engaging pictures and descriptions. Urban planning is a dynamic area for study with creative career opportunities. Students can also learn about community-supported agriculture (CSA) through Local Harvest to learn how rural communities link with urban ones.

The Global Gallery and Performing Arts Center: New Forms and Fusions

Big idea: Contemporary artists worldwide can express their ideas and feelings through new artistic forms and fusions made possible through digital media and global connectivity.

Essential questions: How are artists sharing their work globally? What form of artistic expression best supports my message?

Translation into practice: New forms of expression like composing music digitally, using computer-assisted design programs, and streaming video enable our learners to express themselves and share their work through a wider array of media to an even wider array of observers. Probably one of the most striking changes in the 21st century has been our ability to immediately access global communities of artists and their work. Embracing both classical collections and the avant-garde, the Google Art Project lets students see paintings and visual works from every corner of the world instantly as well as "walk through" any room in a museum or other structure using the building floor plan (www.google .com/culturalinstitute/project/art-project?hl=en).

Consider the remarkably wide range of visual arts from around the world available at Artsy, ranging from assemblage to chiaroscuro to graffiti to typographic photography (http://artsy.net). Students can peruse creations from artists throughout the world for inspiration and new cultural perspectives.

Digital media has also made musical style and innovations available to new, expansive audiences. In addition to iTunes, MediaMonkey, and CopyTrans, there are active professional organizations that can open up the global performing arts experience. The International Society for Contemporary Music (ISCM), which began in 1923, has members throughout the world and supports global connections between composers and performers. Each year, ISCM sponsors World Music Days—dynamic platforms for both performers and audiences (www.iscm .org). Major music festivals, such as South by Southwest (SXSW) held annually in Austin, Texas, are live-streamed worldwide, providing a common venue for meeting and sharing through Twitter feeds and blog posts. Digital music composition provides a vehicle for self-expression, and music educators throughout the world are attempting to integrate tools like Apple's GarageBand, REAPER (www.cockos.com/reaper), or UJAM SongCruncher (www.ujam.com) into their curriculum.

Our students can view the work of young choreographers throughout the world through websites like MOMIX (www.mosespendleton.com/works.html) and the

Nederlands Dans Theater (www.ndt.nl), or join a dancing event throughout the world via Dance Anywhere (www.danceanywhere.org/locations/2013). Aspiring student choreographers can film their own compositions and share them online. Curriculum planners can embrace these opportunities and employ them in an integrated fashion in all subjects. For example, the Kennedy Center is the home of ARTSEDGE (http://artsedge.kennedy-center.org), which provides schools with a wealth of materials to fuse the arts into all academic subjects with free resources and lesson plans.

Lifelong Growth: The Mindful Society and the Mindful Individual

Big idea: An individual's cultivation of thoughtful habits for care of both the mind and the body supports lifelong productivity and a more harmonious society.

Essential questions: How can I become more mindful in my actions with others? How can I support my lifelong growth?

Translation into practice: Ultimately, the study of mindfulness focuses on self-understanding and the cultivation of gravitas. Each child comes to school and socializes, gains and loses friends, goes through rapid changes in his or her body, and takes basic life tests. School often feels like basic training for character development, physical health, and mental well-being. Mindfulness education is fundamental. It is in opposition to mindlessness. Bena Kallick and Arthur Costa's groundbreaking work *Habits of Mind Across the Curriculum* (2009) serves as a basis for schools worldwide to operationalize mindfulness. Their approach is to deliberately engage in the examination of sixteen habits that can sustain and support more meaningful living throughout our lives. The MindUP curriculum (www.thehawnfoundation.org/mindup) provides training and curriculum materials that directly support students' emotional and academic well-being.

Across the world, there are programs to support meditation training, yoga instruction, and thoughtful habits. For example, teachers and learners can connect with the United Kingdom's not-for-profit Mindfulness in Schools Project (called "dot.b"; http://mindfulnessinschools.org), the Institute for Mindfulness South Africa (www.mindfulness.org.za), the Istituto Italiano per la Mindfulness (Italian Institute for Mindfulness; www.istitutomindfulness.com/en), or France's Association pour le Développement de la Mindfulness (Association for the Development of Mindfulness; www.association-mindfulness.org). U.S. public schools have seen an increase in formal instruction in yoga and meditation as a means of achieving focus and balance. In *Teaching Tolerance*, Lisa Ann Williamson (2012) notes that in schools with yoga as a regular part of the program, there are "fewer fights and arguments among students; better student decision-making; increased self-awareness and self-esteem; improved concentration and retention; and more efficient use of class time."

Found in Translation: Second Language Learners Unite

Big idea: Acquiring competence in a language other than one's own supports deeper levels of communication and cultural understanding.

Essential questions: How does acquiring a second language impact my understanding of other people? How can I communicate effectively in a second language?

Translations into practice: Increased attention to world language instruction is a major need as the Committee for Economic Development (2006) notes—

> To confront the twenty-first century challenges to our economy and national security, our education system must be strengthened to increase the foreign language skills and cultural awareness of our students. America's continued global leadership will depend on our students' abilities to interact with the world community both inside and outside our borders. (p. 1)

Knowing a second language is beneficial for any student. Whether a young girl from Peru immigrates to Massachusetts and studies English or a high school sophomore in Utah enrolls in a Mandarin Chinese class, expanding linguistic capability is powerful. The American Council on the Teaching of Foreign Languages (www.actfl.org) makes a concerted effort to bring language instruction to the forefront of school policy decisions. The long-standing view is that the sooner children are introduced to a second language, the easier it is for them to successfully acquire language facility.

One obvious way to connect learners is through direct point-to-point Skype or Google Hangout interactions using the second language. For example, a ninth-grade high school class in Portland, Oregon, studying Japanese might regularly interact with a high school in Kyoto, Japan, studying English. The teachers can record and review these sessions. There are other levels of interaction; rather than simply practicing language, students can share perspectives on the challenges of acquiring another language in a metacognitive look at language acquisition. Another option might be participating in projects, such as 100 People: A World Portrait (www.100people.org), in which schools share a common global focus and compare their experiences in a second language. Newspaper Map (http://newspapermap.com) is a particularly compelling site where students choose an issue, locate newspapers at almost any location worldwide, translate an article into one of thirty different languages, and then compare it with an article about the same issue from another newspaper in another country. The opportunity is there for the second language learner to translate the article into the language he or she is studying.

Global Lessons on Education: What We Can Learn From the Finns

Big idea: A country's educational systems reflect its values in the way it deploys resources to educate children.

Essential question: What can we learn from the Finns about learning?

Translation into practice: The contemporary teacher or administrator is knowledgeable about global perspectives in the field of education. Even as we attempt to expand our curriculum, assessment, and instruction, we easily overlook the systems and methodologies of other countries. Teachers, students, and administrators could begin an interdisciplinary study by viewing the film study *The Finland Phenomenon* (Compton & Faust, 2011; www.2mminutes.com/films /finland-phenomenon.asp). This provocative and carefully crafted documentary has stimulated discussion and debate worldwide. After viewing the film, a natural follow-up would be to read *Finnish Lessons: What Can the World Learn From Educational Change in Finland?* (Sahlberg, 2011). In his book, Pasi Sahlberg writes:

> Finland has been able to transform its educational system from something elitist, unknown, and inefficient into a paragon of equity and efficiency. Finland is also a rare case among the OECD countries that have been able to improve their educational performance as measured by international indicators and student achievement tests. Furthermore, many foreign visitors have been particularly surprised to find out that teaching has become the number one profession among young Finns—above medicine and law—and that primary teacher education in Finnish universities is one of the most competitive choices of study. (p. 5)

Inquiry into global education case studies could be a fascinating collaborative book or film study with both faculty and students together investigating what knowledge might be transferred to our own schools. Students might create a wiki to discuss the case study and perhaps engage a school in Finland in the discussion.

Conclusion

Twenty-first century learners need 21st century teachers to engage in a dynamic global learning environment. Global literacy should focus on a robust examination of:

- People and places through academic study
- Contemporary interdisciplinary global issues
- Physical geography vernacular
- Digital tools for accessing information
- Class-to-class communication using virtual applications

This kind of progressive world can seem daunting, but the alternative is to slip backward. As educators, we must—above all—be learners and be willing to revise curriculum pathways, expand our instructional pedagogy, and engage learners with the new literacies. Interdisciplinary inquiry into timely and essential global issues is a commitment to engage learners in a dynamic investigation of their future. Instead of traveling backward in time, we should be moving forward with them.

References and Resources

Asimov, I. (1982). *Asimov's biographical encyclopedia of science and technology* (Rev. ed.). Garden City, NY: Doubleday.

Association for Media Literacy. (1989). *Media literacy resource guide.* Toronto, Ontario, Canada: Ministry of Education.

Boix Mansilla, V. B., & Jackson, A. (2011). *Educating for global competence: Preparing our youth to engage the world.* New York: Asia Society.

Committee for Economic Development. (2006). *Education for global leadership: The importance of international studies and foreign language education for U.S. economic and national security.* Washington, DC: Author.

Compton, R. A. (Executive Producer), & Faust, S. (Director). (2011). *The Finland phenomenon: Inside the world's most surprising school system* [Motion picture]. United States: True South Studios.

Conant, E. (2012). *Russia's booming nuclear industry.* Accessed at http://pulitzercenter .org/reporting/russia-nuclear-energy-construction-novovoronezh-elemash-reactor on November 8, 2012.

Council of Chief State School Officers. (2010). *EdSteps: Collecting work samples for global competence.* Accessed at http://edsteps.org/CCSSO/SampleWorks/Global Competence.pdf on August 23, 2012.

Facing the Future. (2013). *Exploring global issues: Social, economic, and environmental interconnections.* Seattle, WA: Author.

Geography Education Standards Project. (1994). *Geography for life: National Geography Standards.* Washington, DC: National Geographic Research & Exploration. Accessed at https://netforum.avectra.com/eweb/DynamicPage.aspx ?Site=Test%20One&WebCode=GeographyStandards on June 10, 2013.

Gopnik, A. (2012, October 29). Faces, places, spaces: The renaissance of geographic history. *The New Yorker.* Accessed at www.newyorker.com/arts/critics/atlarge/2012 /10/29/121029crat_atlarge_gopnik on June 6, 2013.

Heffron, S. G., & Downs, R. M. (Eds.). (2012). *Geography for life: National Geography Standards, 2nd ed.* Washington, DC: National Council for Geographic Education.

Jacobs, H. H. (Ed.). (1989). *Interdisciplinary curriculum: Design and implementation.* Alexandria, VA: Association for Supervision and Curriculum Development.

Jacobs, H. H. (Ed.). (2010). *Curriculum 21: Essential education for a changing world.* Alexandria, VA: Association for Supervision and Curriculum Development.

Kallick, B. O., & Costa, A. L. (Eds.). (2009). *Habits of mind across the curriculum: Practical and creative strategies for teachers.* Alexandria, VA: Association for Supervision and Curriculum Development.

Léautier, F. (Ed.). (2006). *Cities in a globalizing world: Governance, performance, and sustainability.* Washington, DC: World Bank.

Llana, S. M. (2012). *Former Rio slums attract hip Europeans looking for cheap housing.* Accessed at http://pulitzercenter.org/reporting/brazil-rio-slums-european-immigrants -economy-housing-vidigal on November 8, 2012.

Maira, S. (2004). *Imperial feelings: Youth, culture, citizenship, and globalization.* In M. M. Suárez-Orozco & D. B. Qin-Hilliard (Eds.), *Globalization: Culture and education in the new millennium* (pp. 203–234). Berkeley: University of California Press.

Meadows, D. H. (1990, May 31). State of the village report. *The Global Citizen.* Accessed at www.redrat.net/thoughts/global_village.htm on August 23, 2013.

Ontario Ministry of Education. (1997). *Media literacy resource guide.* Toronto, Ontario, Canada: Author.

Sahlberg, P. (2011). *Finnish lessons: What can the world learn from educational change in Finland?* New York: Teachers College Press.

Smith, K. D. (1996). Why theory in the history of cartography? *Imago Mundi: The International Journal for the History of Cartography, 48*(1), 198–203.

Stewart, V. (2012). *A world-class education: Learning from international models of excellence and innovation* [Kindle version]. Accessed at www.amazon.com on August 19, 2013.

Trinity College of Arts and Sciences. (n.d.). *Languages at Duke.* Accessed at http://trinity.duke.edu/languages on November 7, 2012.

Washington Center. (2008). *Outcomes and rubrics: Sustainability learning outcomes—Curriculum for the bioregion imitative sustainability learning outcomes.* Olympia, WA: Evergreen State College.

Wikipedia. (n.d.). *File:Babylonian Maps.JPG.* Accessed at http://en.wikipedia.org/wiki/File:Baylonianmaps.JPG#file on November 6, 2012.

Williamson, L. A. (2012). Yoga in public schools. *Teaching Tolerance, 42*(51), 27–28.

Unger, E. (1996). *Imago Mundi: The International Journal for the History of Cartography, 48,* 209.

United Nations Department of Economic and Social Affairs Population Division. (2012). *World urbanization prospects: The 2011 revision.* New York: Author

Index

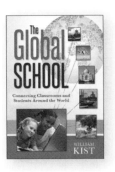

The Global School
By William Kist

Prepare students for an increasingly flat world where diverse people from divergent cultures learn and work together rather than in isolation. Learn specific steps to globalize your classroom and encourage higher-order thinking, all wrapped in a 21st century skills framework. **BKF570 EKF186**

21st Century Skills
Edited by James Bellanca and Ron Brandt

Examine the Framework for 21st Century Learning from the Partnership for 21st Century Skills as a way to re-envision learning in a rapidly evolving global and technological world. Learn why these skills are necessary, which are most important, and how to best help schools include them. **BKF389 EKF035**

Bringing Innovation to School
By Suzie Boss

Activate your students' creativity and problem-solving potential with breakthrough learning projects. Across all grades and content areas, student-driven, collaborative projects will teach students how to generate innovative ideas and then put them into action. **BKF546 EKF132**

Creating a Digital-Rich Classroom
By Meg Ormiston

Design and deliver standards-based lessons in which technology plays an integral role. This book provides a research base and practical strategies for using web 2.0 tools to create engaging lessons that transform and enrich content. **BKF385 EKF076**

Solution Tree | Press

a division of

Solution Tree

Visit solution-tree.com or call 800.733.6786 to order.

Wait! Your professional development journey doesn't have to end with the last pages of this book.

We realize improving student learning doesn't happen overnight. And your school or district shouldn't be left to puzzle out all the details of this process alone.

No matter where you are on the journey, we're committed to helping you get to the next stage.

Take advantage of everything from **custom workshops** to **keynote presentations** and **interactive web and video conferencing**. We can even help you develop an action plan tailored to fit your specific needs.

Let's get the conversation started.

Call 888.763.9045 today.

solution-tree.com